Second Edition, May 2018   **Brexit due 29 March 2019**

Lord Kerr of Kinlochard, the author of Article 50 of the Lisbon Treaty, in an e-mail to the author of 17 December 2017, had this to say about this book and how the United Kingdom can and should remain a member of the European Union:

"You make the argument very well... I am still firmly of the view that the question is still open.... (there are) Leavers who now regret the June 2016 result, but wrongly believe that the die is cast, the Rubicon crossed, and there can be no going back. The Brexiteers like to maintain that we couldn't withdraw the Prime Minister's 29 March letter: in a lecture on 10 November ... I tried to explain that this is entirely untrue: if we want to change our mind, we can, and with no price to pay. We owe it to our children not to give up."

[The full text of Lord Kerr's lecture of 10 November 2017 is at p. 196 with French and German translations]

The Four Brexiteers
And the Fracturing of the West

Presidents Trump and Putin, Mr Rupert Murdoch, and Prime Minister Theresa May : the how and why of Brexit and the populist phenomenon

by John Pedler

former British diplomat, now a diplomatic consultant based in France
website: dipconsult.blogspot.fr, dipconsult@hotmail.com

For all those under 25 who voted on 8 June 2017

'Halt Brexit Now'

Lord Kerr of Kinlochard GCMG author of Article 50 of the Lisbon Treaty, former Head of the UK's Diplomatic Service. His lecture of 10 November 2017 explaining how this can be achieved is at page 196 together with French and German translations

"There are extremely serious consequences of leaving the single market and it hasn't been explained to the British people"

Michel Barnier,
European Chief Negotiator for Brexit, 2 September 2017

Guide to contents

THE ARGUMENT: INTRODUCING BREXIT AND POPULISM

============================

What this short book is about:

The reasons why the UK must 'Halt Brexit Now' and how it could be avoided so freeing the UK to play its vital role in the struggle to roll back populism in the UK, the EU, US and Russia - all now threatening to fracture the unity of the West.

Why the Dedication - and Roger Cohen 9 June 2017 (NYT)

At the 8 June 2017 General Election the under 25s voted in unprecedented numbers against the Conservatives and Brexit. They have become aware that their European future is being stolen by middle aged politicians who have lost touch with those they rule. Not one of those 'came out' against Brexit and only Labour stood for social justice. Of the under 20s voters 75% chose 'remain' at the referendum.

What is so remarkable is that these young people (let's include the under 35s) had no support. We tried hard to get some lead celebrities to 'come out' against Brexit to express the frustrations of their young admirers, none did; we tried to get President Obama and Senator Bernie Sanders to intervene in favour of the EU as they did at the French Presidential election in April/May this year - they didn't. We tried to get some of those those with most to lose from Brexit like financiers in the City of London to 'come out': they didn't. Yet nearly a quarter of the UK's GDP (22%) is generated by The City of London. It is the EU's major financial centre thanks largely to the UK banks having 'financial passporting rights' enabling them to operate throughout the EU: most of this is at risk with Brexit. We tried to persuade the key American media to support the opposition to UK Prime Minister Mrs. Theresa May: but CNN, the New York Times, and the Washington Post had all swallowed the May slogan: 'Brexit is inevitable' and wouldn't. Yet it is a vital interest of the United States that the UK avoid Brexit and do all it can to bolster the European Union as the remaining bastion of democracy.

So the under 25s alone and with no backing suceeded by adding their voice to deny Mrs. May a majority and at last there is an opportunity for the UK to forsake Brexit and be free to play its vital role in preserving democracy as part of an EU assailed now by Putin, Trump, and May and by the flood of refugees following the destabilisation of the Middle East by the US and the UK as long ago as 2003.

As for the older generation – the over 50s, a majority of whom favour leaving the EU – they are largely responsible for the UK's current 'addiction' to Brexit. That is well described by New York Times columnist Roger Cohen (9 June 2017). Because of the humour, I have chosen to quote his piece from much other foreign pessimism about Brexit:

'For a long time I could not bring myself to write about the British election. Trump-coddling, self-important, flip-flopping Theresa May, ensconced at 10 Downing Street without ever being elected prime minister, was going to sweep to her hard-Brexit victory and take the country down her little England rabbit hole.

'There were more important things to think about, like the end of the American century in 2017, one hundred years after the Bolshevik Revolution. A boorish clown named Donald Trump brought down the curtain.

'In Britain, anyway, there was no story: the June 8 vote would be a formality. The Labour Party was in meltdown, having exited the Blairite middle ground for leftist orthodoxy under Jeremy Corbyn. The British, their ludicrous vote to leave the European Union gradually sinking in, had morphed into sheep. May would get her mandate to do her worst, with Boris Johnson, a foreign secretary who long since forsook any claim to be taken seriously, cheering her on..... Of all the obscene spectacles one has had to endure over the past several months, the worst has been that of the United States and Britain — their finest hour but a wan memory ....'

10

How this book is arranged

The Four Brexiteers is an attempt to provide the basic information about Brexit and populism which the British have been denied by the almost exclusively pro-Brexit UK media and by the 'Brexit is inevitable' stance of the US media. It is not intended for other foreign affairs 'gurus' – hence the rather fun title. So I've tried to make this 'remainers' view of Brexit a quick easy read (the first essential part is just 48pp) even though, in our globalised world, it's none too easy to follow the multiple interconnections linking one subject to a host of others. In the second part the supporting documents - inevitably there is repetition because a number of the items I have used often overlap.

At present, end May 2018, perhaps the greatest difficulty in moving towards 'Halting Brexit' are polls which suggest that voters more or less hold to their 2016 referendum vote whether 'Yes' or 'No' – though the most recent polls already show a modest majority in favour of 'remaining'. This dents the pro-Brexit media claim that 'Brexit is the will of the British people and must be respected', or to quote Prime Minister Mrs. Theresa May – "a sovereign decision taken by the British people". This makes all the more important, as Michel Barnier's quote on the title page emphasises, the need to inform UK politicians and public that Brexit can be avoided - a fact that both the UK and the US media fails to discuss. The Four Brexiteers is an effort to correct this self-imposed censorship by the UK media. Once the UK's predicament in today's new world is widely understood the way will be open to halting Brexit.

So this book is not a pessimist's complaint about how 'all is lost' - it is a message of hope. It is possible, even likely, that some politician will be bold enough to lead the UK in ditching Brexit well before it happens. There is no need to let the famous Article 50 of the Lisbon Treaty stand in the way – Lord Kerr's lecture of 10 November 2017, p196. In any case both the UK and the EU have the strongest reasons for avoiding Brexit and national interest usually trumps international law.

For now though, the EU has almost given up hope of 'saving' the UK from Brexit – or rather, given up hope of the UK saving itself - and is concentrating on containing populist menace and resolving its other problems now that, with President Trump the US is no longer a reliable leader of the West. There is Climate Destabilisation, defence, relations with Russia, Islamic extremism and the resultant influx of refugees. And there is the reform of the EU, the Euro and debt among other internal issues. For the time being little cooperation on any of these can be expected from the UK.

The four world figures with prime responsibility for Brexit and populism - though each for different reasons - are President Putin of Russia and President Trump of the United States of America, Mr. Rupert Murdoch head of News International – the world's prime purveyor of information - and Prime Minister Mrs. May. Three of them are multi-billionaires – members of that strictly limited group of the immensely rich who lead our world in the first quarter of the 21st Century which some have dubbed 'The Age of the Golden Calf'.

So I consider each in turn, beginning with Mrs. May who is the exception for she and her husband have considerable but no such vast wealth. After her it is logical to follow with Rupert Murdoch before ending with the closely interlinked Trump and Putin. Again there is overlap because of the various ways in which each influences eachother. Indeed I have found it necessary to make some <u>digressions</u> in order to cover points that would otherwise get overlooked.

At first sight the emphasis on Presidents Trump and Putin in a book on Brexit may seem strange, but it is they who have created a new unstable world order which threatens democracy worldwide. And, after Brexit, the United Kingdom without the EU, and the EU without the United Kingdom, would be gravely prejudiced in their effort to meet the many challenges Trump and Putin together represent.

What Trump brings is uncertainty – and uncertainty, in foreign affairs as in business, is anathema. Behind the uncertainty and cliff hanging, there is the professionalism of Trump the builder, expertly swinging his wrecking ball. He knows just where to inflict maximum damage from his first foray in international afairs when he called in question the long standing United States 'One China Policy' – key for China – to his subsequent carefully aimed demolition of the international achievements of the Obama administration. Above all, Trump is aware that his electoral victory is very likely to have been engineered by President Putin and, worse for him, that Putin holds disgraceful 'kompromat' on him. The future of the Trump administration has important implications for the EU as a whole. The UK must not be paralysed, ostrich-like with Brexit, from co-ordinating a response to Russia and ending Putin's 'war by other means' against the EU.

What Putin brings is a well coordinated, carefully planned and executed campaign to fracture Western democracy using all the tools at his disposal (p45): hacking to alter votes, social media (e.g. misinformation through fake Facebook and Twitter accounts), use of Wikileaks to mislead, etc. And all this is also coordinated with military dispositions designed to evoke fear. Here the EU needs to undermine Putin's grip on Russia and forge a much needed all Europe bloc on the world stage - West and East - between the US and China. Not impossible as is shown further on, but requiring the unity of the EU. The UK's weight is indispensable so, with Brexit, it wouldn't be possible to achieve such a more stable new world order: the stakes cannot be higher.

Most of the items in this short book are reports I wrote for my contacts as a diplomatic consultant, in these I have simply put together points made by other observers – in this sense there is nothing new. It is in linking these pieces and sandwiching them between items by others that makes The Four Brexiteers something of a vade mecum both for those who want to know about both Brexit and populism and for those wanting to take action. My aim is to provide information the UK media has not supplied and to correct some of the information that it has supplied.

I believe I have some claim to be the author. I worked to aid the various proponents of 'remain' from 2015 when David Cameron became Prime Minister with the intent of holding a referendum on UK membership of the EU. So I was a player in all four campaigns (to date) of the Brexit drama. The first was the referendum campaign itself; the second was the litigation which got the High Court declaration that the UK is a parliamentary democracy; the third was the resultant parliamentary campaign in the New Year 2017 to deny Mrs May as Prime Minister May sole authority to invoke Article 50. The fourth campaign, after parliamentary opposition to Article 50 collapsed on 13 March, sought to deny Mrs. May a majority at the General Election that she had unexpectedly called for 8 June. There is much in this book about Russia and the West: UK/EU/US/Russia relations have been a special study of mine since my time in the British Foreign Service (now the Diplomatic Service).

UK Prime Minister Mrs. Theresa May. Ending the unity of the EU

The most devastating effect of the UK's march to Brexit has been the knock on effect for other EU members harbouring voices for 'leave'. Before the UK's referendum EU members had little need to be concerned by the comparatively few voices for quitting the Union. But Mrs. May's decision to interpret the referendum result as a definitive call to 'leave' has had an effect in several EU countries including the remaining key members: France and Germany. 'If Britain can leave, so can we' goes the thinking. In France 'leave' is gaining support despite the containment of Marine Le Pen's National Front in the April/May

14

2017 presidential election And now in Germany the extreme right Alternative for Germany has gained 94 seats in the Bundestag in the 24 September general election ushering in an entirely new balance in German – and thus EU – politics. The AFG exploits the xenophobia following by flood of refugees from Syria a decade after the destabilisation of the Middle East by the 2003 UK/US invasion of Iraq.

Mrs. May was the first to fracture not just EU unity but Western unity. The towering figure of Trump has since put her in the shade as he preaches a return to selfish nationalism worldwide.

While the personalities of the other three Brexiteers and the motivation of two of them (Putin and Murdoch) are fairly well defined Mrs. May is an enigma – why, once elected leader of the deeply divided parliamentary Conservative Party, did she decide to invoke Article 50 putting the UK on the one way street to an unknowable Brexit? Unknowable because, whatever she may claim, the Brexit the UK gets is what the other 27 countries unanimously agree – and they well may not, leaving the UK with no exiting agreement. Mrs May is quite right in her proclamation that 'Brexit means Brexit' for the damage will be done whether it's the so-called 'hard' Brexit, without access to the Common Market, or the 'soft Brexit' with it.

She and 'her few, her band of Brexit brothers' actually achieving Brexit is now admitted to be the greatest peacetime challenge Britain has faced. Which begs the question – why take on such a daunting task when the benfits are so uncertain?

Mrs. May has to come first for consideration as the only one of these four who, on 29 March 2017 was able to fire the Brexit starting gun. In nearly a year from the 2016 purely advisory referendum until the June 2017 General Election, she did not, as is expected of a prime minister after a non-binding referendum, set out to ensure the vital international interests of the UK while striving to carry the country with her - especially after such a close referendum result 51.89% to 48.11%. The difference was only 1,269,501. If all the 2m odd British nationals living in the continental EU had had the vote – which most did not - 'remain' could well have won, and if all the 5m odd British passport holders living outside the UK – those with most to lose from Brexit – had had the vote 'remain' would have won by a landslide.

Now that she has invoked Article 50 and dealt such a forceful blow not just to the vital national interests of both the UK and the EU, but also – pace President Trump - to the true interests of the US, and to all the world's other democracies now struggling to survive in a hostile environment, she – unlike the other three - has no further role to play. Her one arrow has hit its target to devastating effect, but she has no more in her quiver. If she survives as Prime Minister (and this seems most uncertain) and gets her Brexit, history will decide whether she will go down as the most disastrous British prime minister since Neville Chamberlain who was duped by Hitler – or since Tony Blair who joined US President G. W. Bush in the invasion of Iraq in 2003 so destabilising the Middle East, eventually getting us the Syrian civil war and the mass refugee influx to Europe which so helped inflate the 'leave' vote. (A lot of UK voters were already worried by the Bush/Blair destabilisation of the Middle East and its international consequences. So believed 'leave's' bogus claim that the EU would be swamped by Turkey's accession with its 75 million Muslims!)

Indeed, the most striking absence from all four of those Brexit campaigns has been the dire international implications of Article 50 and of Brexit itself. They have have been almost totally ignored.

In those last days before Mrs. May 'irrevocably' invoked Article 50 many of us were hoping that the House of Lords with its great majority of 'remain' voters and its members with their tenure for life, would stand up to the Commons to delay such controversial legislation - MPs only hold a maximum tenure of 5 years before another election and therefore often take a short term view of legislation to the detriment of the UK's longer interest. So, with the Commons poised to authorise the use of Article 50, as one wag put it "salvation comes from the Lords".

But the Lords, like the Commons collapsed and Mrs. May got the Article 50 authorisation she demanded in an undignified rush in both Commons and Lords on the same day – 13 March 2017. The Commons vote was 331 to 286, a majority of no more than 48. The Lords acquiesced to the Commons decision by 274 to 118: a far greater majority of 156 - and this although the great majority of the Lords like the MPs in the Commons voted 'remain' in the referendum. This precedent for following a Commons vote, even though seriously misconceived, must put in doubt the Lords as an effective second, revisionary, chamber able to delay a misguided decision of the Commons long enough for second thoughts.

Mrs May, with only that handful of supporters, thus appears to have won that prerequisite for populists – weakening so far as possible the people's representatives so diminishing their essential role between the voter and those exercising power.

Many have pointed out that direct election of a President is far more dangerous for democracy than a parliamentary system where the people elect Members of Parliament who are far more likely to choose the best leader – Prime Minister or leader of the opposition. But, in the UK, that assurance has been eroded in both parties with the addition of non-MPs who can effect the outcome and get an entirely unsuitable leader. In 2015 Labour's leader, Ed Miliband, changed the voting rules to allow anyone to vote for leader by paying £3! That explains the choice of Jeremy Corbyn who, by insisting on Brexit, removed Labour as an effective opposition to Conservative Prime Minister Mrs. May.

The rules for the election of a Conservative leader are not that dissimilar – in that you had to have been a member of the Conservative party before the nominations were opened up on the 29 June 2016 in order to be able to vote in the contest. And you only had to have been a member for three months before the time the voting ends.

It seems that practically no one in England or even in Wales realises what is common talk on the continent – that the British have done what used to be most un-British – let down their friends and allies in their hour of need to side instead with Putin and Trump, the EU's enemies: NATO itself is targetted by Trump. A 'renversement des alliances'.

How did politicians and popular opinion succumb to the Brexit's siren call? And why did Mrs. May choose populism and hard to win Brexit?
She had the opportunity to take on the far easier task of healing the country's division by explaining that after this advisory referendum she would examine the referendum campaign and then act in the best interests of the UK. And, that clearly meant supporting our friends and allies in the EU and the world - certainly not deserting them.

After experiencing Mrs. May's high-handed obstinacy and refusal to listen to opponents a few years ago, I suggest the May enigma may best be explained by her finding herself, after her election as leader – and thus Prime Minister - on 11 July 2016 (when she was still considered a 'Remain' supporter) with an unexpected opportunity to embrace populism thereby much enhancing her own unfettered ability to shape events. (165 Conservative MPs, most of whom had been 'remain', voted for her of a total of 282, while only 117 voted against her plus Brexit supporter Michael Gove). This hypothesis seems to me to fit the picture judging by her subsequent actions.

Mrs. May or any other Prime Minister – to obtain general acquiesence for 'remain' - would need to promise to provide the necessary funding to take credible measures to assuage the very real grievances of so many 'leavers'.

Since the 29 March invocation of Article 50 I have found rather less bigotry and an increased readiness to discuss, though extremist leavers still represent a physical threat. (One exmple: Mrs. Gina Miller, whose litigation which led to a declartion of the supremacy of Parliament is deeply resented by extremist 'leavers', has to have police protection because of threats against her life). Indeed many of them, less certain about their vote, have come to share that fatalistic acceptance of some senior politicians. For instance one 'leaver', who claims his view is shared by many, explained to me that he had voted 'leave' "because of the lack of democratic control of the Commission – it does what it wants, there is no democracy to check it. The EU needed reform - but that is impossible with so much bureaucratic intransigence. The EU parliament should be curbing that - but it's a sheep not a wolf. If voters had real power and your MEP was someone it would be different. That's what a lot of us say. Well, whether our vote was right or wrong we've just got to get on with it". Curious, that phrase 'we've got to get on with it' is also used by 'remainers'. So is: 'it's all over now, it's no use thinking about it: we've just got to make the best of it'. Initiated by Mrs. May and fanned by the UK press there is still much incivility and belittlement, for example use of the buzz term 'remoaners' for those against Brexit.

But talking to both 'remain' and 'leave' you get the impression that more important than economics, democracy, and 'independence' in determining 'leave' votes is that run down of the UK's social services since the cuts due to the austerity campaign, as compared with the other major EU countries like France – this chimes well with the 'leavers' emotive slogan 'take back control'. I have personal experience of this and so can vouch for the lamentable deterioration of the UK's Social Services as depicted in Ken Loache's *palme d'or* winning 'I Daniel Blake'. Another major grievance is the advent of 'zero hour contracts': for more important than actual wages is security of employment. And too often forgotten is the financial loss ordinary people suffered from the 2007 financial collapse.

Indeed the entire edifice of Social Welfare and the National Health Service, once the pride of Britain, is now so overburdened by demand and so underfunded because of a badly managed austerity campaign by the last Labour and Conservative governments that there is not enough of either to go round for the British let alone for foreigners whether from the EU or anywhere else. Badly managed because, even when obliging austerity elsewhere, there are some things that need more to be spent on them, not less. Think of the police and the security services, as well as health and welfare – they were cut too, greatly hampering those services' response to much increased threats from terrorists.

On a lighter note – two tales of 'leavery': in Peterborough a man who had voted 'leave' complained a few days later "why are all those Pakis still here?" not realising that it is only people from other EU countries who would be affected, not those from the Indian sub-continent. This all to common confusion, is just one example of how those who know less are dragging those who know more down the slippery slope to Brexit. Studies suggest that, both in the US election and in the UK referendum, most of those who voted for Trump in the US or for Brexit in the UK tend to lack the standard of education of those who voted for Mrs. Clinton or for 'remain'. Rather more humorous is a report from Birmingham that quite a few of those from India and Pakistan voted 'leave' because of commercial competition from continental Europeans!

<u>Mrs May and the petition signed by 1.86m against a State Visit by President Trump – reckless on the part of a Prime Minister</u>

Here it is worth observing that, in the absence of an effective opposition in the Commons the proper focus for dissatisfaction with government, the only undeniable mass opposition to Mrs. May has been the 1.86m signatory petition against Trump being invited for a state visit to the UK.

The House of Commons debate on the petition on 20 February 2017 provided the first widely supported opportunity to protest against Mrs. May's determination to use the Royal prerogative (equivalent to a US 'executive order') to make decisions of the first importance. The first was her insistence that she could, acting alone, invoke Article 50 of the Lisbon Treaty – which the UK Supreme Court denied her. And and then there was that invitation extended on her own authority to President Trump to make a state visit to the UK without taking advice or allowing the normal delay in establishing the invitee's suitability.

Yet Mrs. May undoubtedly knew, as the UK general public knew, of Trump's boorish character which would be offensive to a large proportion of the British public let alone to the 90 year old Queen held in high regard by most of the nation. And more importantly, as Prime Minister Mrs. May must have known of the 35 page Orbis intelligence report at (full text as published, p142) compiled by a former British Secret Intelligence Service officer about Mr. Trump's top aides' relations with Russian intelligence during the 2016 presidential campaign. A report which was considered to be of such great significance by all 17 American intelligence services as to merit presentation last December both to then President Obama and to then President elect Trump. It was obvious to observers that, once subjected to scrutiny, this had the potential to shake the Trump presidency to the core bringing disrepute on the President himself.

In these circumstances Mrs. May's issue of an invitation to him on her sole authority right after his inauguration can only be described as reckless. And for what? An attempt to ensure for her Brexit policy the assurance of that President Trump – another Brexiteer – would continue the US much vaunted 'special relationship' with the UK? He has'nt. This incident raises serious doubts about Mrs May's competence as the UK's leader. It demonstrated the profound widespread dissatisfaction with her which continues, though it then, and still does, lack a focus. No politician and few organisations are yet ready to exploit this distrust of Mrs. May and her determination to achieve Brexit.

There is one point which is all but entirely neglected but which needs to be made: likely Russian interference in the 2016 referendum and the June 2017 General Election. Here's a short note on this which I wrote early in the 8 June election campaign:

'Putin is still very much at large. Despite US intelligence experts warning publicly that Russia is likely to be interfering with this UK election in favour of Mrs. May, as he did only weeks ago with the French Presidential Election, there has been no UK government warning. That is a grave dereliction of duty. It is much to be hoped that our legitimate last minute surprises will be far more effective than any last minute illegitimate surprise that Putin may have in store. He has a far greater interest in ensuring Mrs. May's majority than he did in supporting Marine Le Pen in France. If Brexit is gone, so is all the work Putin has done to undermine the unity of the EU. That would make him weaker at home and much help those many Russians who would like to restore Europe as a whole to its proper place on the world scene, culturally, diplomatically, and for defence.

'An informed guess is that he is using hacker Fancy Bear's highly sophisticated algorithm, used to great effect in last year's US presidential election, to identify US states where the vote was likely to be close, and concentrate on these with fake information and other tools at his disposal to sway the vote in favour of Trump. This same algorithm is likely to be in operation to pinpoint constituencies in the UK where a close vote is likely and then using those other tools to favour a May win in those.

'Whether, or if so with what success, Putin interfered with the UK 2016 referendum cannot be known in the absence of an expert enquiry'. (See p. 45 for Cambridge Analytica's role now revealed).

Mr. Rupert Murdoch – a preliminary word

A digression on populism

The media, of which Mr. Murdoch is the world's information mogul, is so important to an understanding of both Brexit and populism – particularly in the US – that any consideration of Mr. Murdoch must involve major digressions:

First of all, it is worth considering the five preconditions needed for a successful populist grab for power. Preconditions which enabled Mr. Murdoch to create his 'alternative reality' in both the US and the UK.

To start of with, a considerable section of the population must share an underlying resentment that is not being addressed by the people's representatives who must have largely lost touch with their supporters. (Both Republicans and Democrats in the US, both Labour and Conservatives in the UK, and President Yeltsin's regime in Russia). In the US and the UK there were many who had been left behind by globalisation and international competition. In the case of the US the November 2016 election was, in large part, a last stand to 'keep America white' although overt racism has in large measure gone underground. (see Paul Ktugman p107). In the UK, for many over 50s, it was a harking back to a bygone era when 'Britain was British': a reaction to those foreign workers crowding out British from jobs and social benefits. As I say, in the name of austerity, these had been pretty savagely cut when they should have been the one exception needing greater, not less, funding even if strict austerity was to be pursued elsewhere. In Russia what enabled Putin to grab populist power was the widespread perception that the country had no alternative but fight back against neo-conservative US unipolarism (led by Vice

President Cheney) - and specifically US interference in the Ukraine. And that despite even more savage cuts in Russian welfare and incomes.

Secondly, there must be considerable media support for these dissidents – this was the case in the US with Rupert Murdoch's Fox News, radio and press and other outlets; in the UK almost the entire press followed Murdoch in supporting Brexit – or at least did not stand firmly against it. He also has a majority holding in Sky News. The widely respected BBC pulled its punches – apparently fearing a severe cut in its licence fee under May's Conservative government. In Russia an accelerating reduction of media freedom began as Putin returned to the presidency in 2012 whipping up that deep patriotic concern about the Ukraine – Kiev was the 'home' of 'Rus' long before Moscow's ascendency. He highlighted and exploited widespread fear that those US neo-conservatives would end Russia's age-long security and cultural 'special relationship' with the Ukraine. That gave him an ideal opportunity to seize populist power in Russia. Like Mrs. May he chose the hard way of confrontation. He has made himself an anti-EU quasi-dictator against the vital interest of Russia which is to have the closest possible relations with the rest of Europe. There is a French book entitled 'We made Adolf Hitler'. Did the American media, egged on by Rupert Murdoch, 'make' Vladimir Putin without a thought for the EU's vital interest in fostering a strong Europe – east and west – matching the same real identical interest of Russia? Did we western Europeans allow America to loose in Putin that 'tendency for all power to corrupt and for absolute power to corrupt absolutely?'

In all these cases there was no indigenous media loud enough to drown out pro government media. In the case of the UK, there was also that critical lack of US media support for that half of the country struggling to avoid Article 50. This, although the most prestigious elements of the US media well knew of that vital national interest of the US - the avoidance of Brexit to prevent the splintering of the EU.

These – the New York Times, the Washington Post and CNN – have swallowed Mrs May's 'Brexit is inevitable' propaganda uncritically and have persuaded themselves that it would a waste of newsprint to come to the aid of the opposition. If the US media had forced attention to the all but totally ignored world-wide implications of Brexit there is a good chance that English politicians and public would, before too late, have awoken to the dire international aspect. My appeal about this got a sympathetic response from a senior member of the Washington Post. To no avail – the Editorial director stuck to the paper's assessment of Brexit inevitability.

The same proved true of the International New York Times. I managed to get this letter published, 20 September 2016: **Brexit: 'Inevitable or Not': my letter to the International New York Times, 20 September 2016** 'Steven Erlanger [NYT Bureau Chief in London] sets out the many daunting decisions faced by Prime Minister Theresa May as she leads Britain toward Brexit, which is considered all but universally inevitable, both by British politicians of all parties, and other European Union leaders. However, in the final quarter of this year, there will be a last chance to avoid Brexit: when the High Court — and likely, the Supreme Court of the United Kingdom — will hear the challenges to Mrs. May's claim that she alone can invoke Article 50. (She has said she will probably do so early in 2017, without a prior vote in Parliament). As it stands, 479 out of 637 MPs who declared their position should be enough of a clear majority to block the invocation of Article 50. But that majority is undoubtedly so ingrained with the mistaken belief that to oppose Brexit would be to flout democracy because — by just 52 percent — "the British people have spoken." So now it falls to the media to inform those in Britain, the European Union and the world who believe it to be possible that Brexit could be avoided'.

My subsequent follow up submission was declined. I pointed out that the subject was of considerable importance to the US as well as to the

UK and the US and that the paper should surely find someone with more clout to make the essential point. My same text, only slightly edited, was published by France's Le Monde on 2 November 2016, inter alia eliciting a response from Brussels.

<u>Third</u>: the would-be populist must usurp emotive words like 'democracy', 'the will of the people', 'patriotism' etc., and create his/her 'alternative reality' using 'fake news' and coming down hard on those who do not accept it. This was successful in the UK and Russia, but in the US freedom of the media under the First Amendment makes it much more difficult to ensure in the longer run. (This technique was, of course, used by the USSR in taking over the word 'peace').

<u>Fourth</u>: the existing legislators must in considerable number be 'pollingticians' more anxious to achieve their own re-election than achieve their country's good. And there must be an element of fear. (This applied to both major parties in the US and the UK. In the UK the House of Lords was itself under threat from reformers as a non-elected chamber and so lacking in determination to delay a decision in the Commons. In Russia the Duma has always lacked power).

<u>Fifth</u>: in these circumstances the populist's repeated claim that he/she is the only one who can put things right comes to be widely believed and he/she becomes the owner of those emotive words. The populist always claims to be able to enhance the standing of his/her country – when in fact they are doing the opposite. (Putin, Mrs May, and Trump all make this false claim to great effect). Having critically weakened the people's representatives, the populist, on coming to power, continues to drum home the message of personally embodying the will of the people. (Trump immediately after his inauguration defined the White House as 'the people's house').

<u>Points mostly neglected by the Murdoch led media</u>

But two factors could upset rule by the populists – one is the possibility that Trump's team can be shown under Trump's leadership to have been in cahoots with Putin's Russia to secure his election. This would have immense consequences. Right now both the House of Representatives and the Senate have separate investigations into what the US intelligence services have learned, and are learning, about this. And Special Counsel Robert Mueller is furnishing both with very substantial ongoing results of his investigations so far apparently providing grounds for impeachment. (The last part of this book deals with the Trump Putin relationship from the beginning of Trump's election campaign, ending with the famous 35 pages of the Orbis Business Intelligence report compiled by the former British Secret Intelligence Service officer Christopher Steele. As I say, this was judged sufficiently compelling by the US's 17 intelligence agencies to warrant its contents being cited when they presented their own assessment to both President Obama and President Elect Trump in December 2016. I added this when I found that many of my political and other contacts involved in foreign affairs have not read it).

The second factor is the growing awareness in the UK of how nebulous the benefits of Brexit would ultimately prove as Mrs. May embarks on her two years of highly complex negotiations with the EU. Somewhere along that 'one way street' to Brexit, parliament will have to enact – it is estimated - seven bills to extricate the UK from the EU. So parliament might yet revolt against Mrs. May's minority Conservative government and the EU be so relieved that, exceptionally, Article 50 could be rolled back and the UK – because of the unique challenges it faces as an EU member - be granted better terms than Mrs. May could achieve from the Commission. That would go some distance in diminishing the international harm already caused by the Article 50 invocation.

How could we in the UK have lost when both Houses at the referendum had overwhelming majorities for 'remain'? It wasn't only Mrs. May, a 'remainer', who turned coat - there were hundreds of turncoats in both Houses egged on by the Brexiteering of Murdoch followed by most of the rest of the English media. Jeremy Corbyn, who led Labour to 'Remain', put on a very different coat when he issued a three line whip ordering Labour MPs to vote for a Conservative Prime Minister invoking Article 50. That split the Labour Party and not only appeared to end real opposition to Mrs. May but simultaneously to end any reasonable hope, by opposing the folly of Brexit, of a Labour comeback, even a 'Halt Brexit' Labour government.

Seeing Corbyn so adamant for Brexit when he, acting alone, had had the power to prevent it by sticking to his former 'remain' stance and leading a united party, it is no wonder that the American media decided that lack of any effective parliamentary opposition meant there was no appreciable opposition to cover! But what a mistake that is when Corbyn, since the 8 June 2017 general election, can credibly expect to become the next Prime Minister except that he is dogged by divisions not only in Labour, but in the electorate over Brexit. Hundreds of us 'remainers' must have contacted him in 2017 begging him to oppose Brexit for the reasons he gave in his remarkable 14 April 2016 speech (full text p186) because it is so little known. With No. 10 as the prize, Corbyn is already showing impatience with Brexit insisting on staying in the Customs Union - a major complication.

But so long as Corbyn does not oppose Brexit there is no real choice for the electorate: two Brexiteers – either Mrs May or Jeremy Corbyn. And Mrs May by exploiting widespread fear of Corbyn's far left agenda is presenting herself as the only possible choice. This of course neglects he fact that it is the House of Commons which decides who is to be Prime Minister – the MP who can win the votes of a majority of MPs. As things are it is most unlikely to be Corbyn - there are others in the wings, Labour's Umunna is one of them.

When Chamberlain was at last seen to have been duped by Hitler there was Churchill in the wings already well prepared to take over on that fateful 10 of May 1940. And Corbyn is certainly no Chuchill. If he does not return to 'remain' there are others, maybe from among those, 'the few', who voted and worked for 'remain' right up to that fateful 29 March 2017 - who will emerge from today's shadows. But whoever it is will have to be prepared to face a drubbing from the English media and even threats requiring police protection. That deters many who would like to see Brexit ditched. But we are hearing that one or two 'celebrities' (many have much more clout than politicians), who hesitated for fear of being the only ones openly to oppose Brexit, may now be ready to 'come out'. They need encouragement and the facts.

If it's not Labour, maybe a new party will be formed uniting the Labour 'few' with the Libdems – and perhaps even with the Conservative 'few.' Or maybe more likely a working coalition of all of them to ditch Brexit?

As already mentioned, Labour or any such grouping will have to agree on **what needs to be put right if they are to carry enough of the country with them in 'remaining'.** That is easier than when the extreme elements 'of leave' were more intimidating than they are now in the autumn of 2017.

One thing I suggest is that any such group makes a point of enquiring into other countries more successful performances than those of the UK. Why do the Swedes, for example, succeed in having a far lower rate of recidivism after a first prison sentence than in the UK? This is particularly important when so many Muslims are 'radicalised' and become devotees of ISIS and Al-quaida when in prison.

One of the main reasons for voting 'leave' – as I've said, but which is all too often forgotten - was the disastrous effect of the 2007 financial collapse on so many. They had to watch resentfully when big banks were saved with publicly funded cash injections. I believe that one area where the UK (and the US) neglected to assuage these grievances, so important for 'leavers', was in failing to study and adopt Germany's 'apprenticeship' programme. Despite 'austerity' which gripped so many countries after the financial collapse, this programme ensured that German workers suffering from globalisation had the opportunity to benefit by this government programme and prepare themselves for the higher technology jobs on offer. Politicians in the UK, and even more the Republicans in the US with their ideology of 'smaller government', missed out on this.

Worse – public education in the UK (and in the US) is well below the standard reached in the post WWII years. It has been left cap in hand about last in the queue for budget disbursements. Yet education is the future for every country and a sine qua non for effective democracy.

And in addition to that, not only is Brexit stealing from our young people their bright future as the Europeans they are - but an absurd limitation on immigrants from other EU countries is set to deprive them of exceptional teachers. Because of the absence of any such restriction after World War II my generation was able to benefit from the best teachers in Europe – notably outstanding Jewish professors who had fled to the UK and so survived the holocaust.

This brings me to the parlous state of many of our finest scientists. That is because finance for the 'cutting edge' of science ensuring the EU's lead in pressing forward the frontiers of knowledge comes not from each country's budgets but a joint EU fund into which each country pays. When last year, after the referendum result, I paid a visit to a professor I know in King's College London who is one of the world's foremost in discovering new applications for DNA with their immense potential (e.g. bio-informatics). I found him planning to move to the continent because he stood to lose his entire income from the

EU's science fund if the UK does divorce the EU. He asked who among those who had voted 'leave' had given one thought to this.

Yes, that coalition of 'the few' or some new party will have a large number of such matters to promise to put right when they appeal to the electorate for support. They need to study, starting now, just what are the wounds that the prospect of Brexit has, and still is, inflicting and how they need to be treated. Should 'the worm turn' they need to be ready if a Halt to Brexit is to be generally accepted.

The first thing needed is to restore the UK's indispensable part as a world player. I have already lamented the way we have abruptly abandoned our friends and allies in an hour of great need and are siding with the enemies of true democracy while flying false democratic colours. And making this 'renversement des alliances' without a thought for them – including the United States our most important and long-standing ally, or any of the others who fought with us in the two world wars. The fact that America so mistakenly chose a wrecker (hardly too strong a word) for a President in highly suspicious circumstances should have led the UK to support the very active opposition to Trump in the US – not, as Mrs. May did, cuddle up to him in a humiliating manner.

Worse, we have become so selfishly engrossed in bulldozing a path to Brexit that we lack the time and resources to retain our position as a prime leader in establishing true democracy not just in our Europe but in the world. Absorbed in Brexit, we are all but paralysed unable to act meaningfully on the world stage. And that, when the act we should play is crucial now starting with the most important of all, Climate Change (or the more accurate Climate Destabilisation, the phrase used by Britain's Sir Crispin Tickell in the 1970s when climate consciousness first began to enter world politics). That is bad enough when the UK possesses some of the world's key leaders in climate science!

UK/EU/US relations with Russia

Here I'll confine myself to one more urgent issue which the UK should be acting with the EU to address – and that is the EU's relations with Russia. As I hope to show in much of this book this is probably more important than anything else – even the calamity in Syria. And that's because Russian action in Syria is bound up with that interference by the US in the Ukraine. Now that US relations with Russia are on hold due to the cloud hanging over President Trump who cannot afford to be seen as in any way favouring Putin, the EU has a rare opportunity to forward its own interest – namely fundamentally improving relations with Russia. There are no longer those neo-conservative ambitions to create that US hegemonic unipolar world.

The problem of course is President Putin – and West takes him at his word when he claims – as populists do - to have the support of some 80% of Russians. Yet the cracks in his popularity have long been visible. As I say, his successful bid to become a populist quasi-dictator depended on gathering behind him even his most determined adversaries by waving the Russian flag, patriotically calling for all Russians to follow him in condemning America's defiance of Russia's vital national interest: preserving its centuries old and very real 'special relationship' with the Ukraine.

But despite that, there are many reasons for Russian dissatisfaction with Putin's internal and foreign policies – austerity beyond anything practiced in the West largely due to the dramatic fall in the cost of oil. On a visit to the pre-glasnost Soviet Union I found that many Russians, through samizdat, radio and other means were as well informed as most of us about what was going on in the outside world. Today, with travelling permitted – provided you have the airfare! – more and more Russians are rediscovering their deep traditional ties with western Europe and resenting the Putin censorship, more efficient than the Tsars', in downplaying the coveted cultural and fraternal and other exchanges that so many Russians yearn for. And today they also have internet search engines and social media to keep them informed.

Indeed, after my own experiences with today's Russians, I do not think it too much to say that that desire for Russia once again to become part of Europe is Putin's Achilles heel. If the EU took the opportunity, now that the US is largely out of the equation, to make a concerted approach to Russia offering the closest possible relationship provided Russia in return dropped its animosity for the EU – and this were publicised effectively - it would be exceedingly difficult for Putin to continue his cyber-war against the unity of Europe, the dream of so many of his people.   But that would be so much easier if the UK, once admired for foreign policy prowess, were there acting with the rest of the EU in such a joint venture to alter much for the better the balance of world power. For that would effectively put all Europe as a bloc between the US and China working for the interest of mankind.

The British attachment to democracy seemed to require acceptance of Brexit. It seemed to be time for the famed British stiff upper lip and, in the name of democracy, for 'remainers' to go down with the ship. A member of the House of Lords and a famed international journalist both told me that they had to accept democracy. It was imperative to 'respect the outcome of the referendum' as 'politically correct.'

Then there's the 'pollingticians' whose profession is to get elected and stay elected. Vicars of Bray accepting the orthodoxy of the day they see their survival as going along with their constituents if a majority voted 'leave' instead of explaining why the UK's interest lies in sticking with the EU and the West. We expect professional competence in almost all walks of from Doctors to train drivers, but not from politicians, a number of whom are extraordinarily ill-informed about the matters they, as our representatives, are expected to deal with - and the consequences of Brexit is one of them.

There's also that supremacy of Mrs. May's influence with the media. Here Murdoch led the pack. The Brexit story boosted circulation but the EU story was a turn off when almost all the press was financially very hard pressed. The 'remain' campaign (Labour and 'official') was lamentably lacking in interest, while 'leave's' was, in the populist manner, titilating but highly misleading. (My first report on Brexit, below p49, describes the deeply flawed referendum campaign).

Despite appeals by foreign affairs professionals, no 'remain' grouping would listen when told that their endless arguments about the economic advantages were indeed dreary and necessarily inconclusive. Yet the real argument for 'remain' was positive, even exciting - the need for the UK to play its role in the EU and the world, taking the lead in reforming the EU and enhancing its influence in world affairs – so urgently needed given the doubts about America's leadership under Trump. Ironically this need for Britain to lead EU reform was best expressed by Jeremy Corbyn in his 'remain' speech of 14 April 2016. [As I said, I have appended this remarkable speech at p184 because it is so little known even by Labour MPs. Yet it is a 'must read' for it represents Labour policy at its best.

There was a virtually complete blackout about foreign affairs – no consideration by politicians, public, or media - both UK and US of the international consequences of Brexit. I myself did all I could to make these known from November 2016 when I had a discussion with Alan Johnson. But neither his Labour 'remain' nor the 'official' remain would accept my (and others) repeated advice to highlight these. The UK press from Guardian to Telegraph via the Independent refused to accept that - as in the past - the media of whatever persuasion, should sometimes allow the expression of views contrary to the owner's policies.

An unexpected and nasty surprise, which may have clinched Brexit, was that refusal of the serious American media to stress and explain that the US has a major interest in avoiding Brexit. This was astonishing - at the top editorial level and among senior reporters the conviction that Brexit was inevitable has risked becoming a self-fulfilling prophecy. So with UK and US media either silent or pro-Brexit even MPs I was in touch with, though opposed to Brexit, were lamentably ill informed about the foreign affairs aspect.

Then there was – and remains – the failure of 'remain' to fully discover and react to the reasons why 'leavers' rejected the EU. Of course one reason was being left behind by globalisation. There was too, for the over 50s, that nostalgic harking back to 'when Britain was British'. Then there was that inability of the social services to meet both UK and foreign requirements. There were also other important concerns which 'remain' largely ignored which are also included under the call to 'Take Back Control' - notably EU common market regulations, excessive bureaucracy, and the supremacy of the European Court of Justice. As regards regulations: all advanced countries have regulations to ensure safety, efficiency, and uniformity. All members of the EU have the same regulations, each country joining in deciding which regulations are imposed and which replaced or amended. Outside the EU the UK would have no say in this – a serious loss when the UK would, like all other countries, have to accept EU regulations when trading with the EU. Then the UK would need to decide on its own regulations which would create problems unless closely based on those of the EU.

As for excessive bureaucracy – this is a major topic in the EU: the Commission itself accepts that it needs rather drastic reform and to correct that democratic deficit: inside the EU the UK would have a major role to play in such imminent major reform, outside it would have none. Supremacy of the European Court of Justice is more complex. Most decisions of the Court present little or no difficulty but there are some decisions, especially those involving human rights, which present major difficulties for some countries, not just the UK.

This has provoked discussion about altering procedure in the case of a country's serious disagreement with a judgment of the ECJ. As a member of the EU the UK would have a major role to play in negotiation about procedural reform on this issue. To sum up: the specious, but so emotionally attractive, slogan 'to take back control' in fact involves a substantial 'loss of control'.

Mr. Rupert Murdoch – a further word

The weakened UK media enabling Mr. Murdoch's leadership.

To conclude this digression: a summary of the reasons why the UK took to Brexit and the role of Mr. Murdoch and the media

Returning to Mr. Murdoch and his role in Brexit, as we have seen, the media has to have been weakened before a populist can take power.

In Mrs May's case the UK's press has for some time been badly stretched financially by internet competition.

The Daily Telegraph, the UK's influential middlebrow broadsheet, was making money partly from Boris Johnson, 'leave's' charismatic TV personality, from his long series of articles trashing Brussels and the EU. But its profits had fallen in 2015 and we hear that its owners, the Barclay brother twins, Sir David and Sir Frederick, had made it plain to Editor Mr. Chris Evans that reversing that trend was what they wanted. So it appears that it was to gain readership that the paper took a determined and persuasive 'leave' position which much helped to persuade quite a number of middle class readers to vote accordingly. The Telegraph, long respected for its unbiased coverage of the news, would not follow its former policy of printing items which disagreed with its editorial line – I know, as a past contributor, I tried persuasion without success.

This drive to avoid losses led several papers to back Brexit because, as I say, that was a gripping story while the dreary 'remain' items arguing that the UK would be better off financially in the EU were a turn off. But this one-sided policy was not confined to the Telegraph, the Express and Mr. Murdoch's Sun and his other outlets. This 'voluntary UK censorship is not that dissimilar to Putin's 'voluntary' censorship!

For Murdoch, arch Brexiteer – who helped Mrs. May more than any others to soften up politicians and people for Brexit – it was different and can be summed up by his reputed words "when I go to Brussels no one listens to me, when I go to London everyone does". He has reportedy claimed that he 'made' the last two British Prime Ministers – Labour's Tony Blair and the Conservatives' David Cameron. With his ownership of top market The Times and The Sunday Times and the UK's circulation leader the tabloid Sun, he to a great extent determined the 'leave' content of the others. And of course Murdoch and his News International are also majority shareholders in Sky News TV widely watched by Britons. Here my attempts to get a fair hearing for those struggling against Brexit brought the accustomed stony silence.

Like the Telegraph's owners, the Daily Mail's owners, a trust ensuring Viscount Rothermere's interests, are reported to have told editor Paul Dacre to keep up the circulation – editorial policy took second place.

More interesting – the Daily Express owned by the controversial Richard Desmond, led him to use highly charged gimmicks to 'up' circulation. He publicised the fact that he had given Nigel Farage's extreme pro-Brexit United Kingdom Independence Party £1m for campaigning. That got the Express a lot of attention! We wait to see the new editorial line now that Desmond has sold the Express to Trinity Mirror, the owners of the anti-Brexit Daily Mirror.

As for the BBC – its political adviser took the US media line assuring me that the BBC would cover opposition to Mrs. May if any turned up.

As I say, those directing the 'Beeb' were – and still are – deeply concerned about the Conservative government's hostility to the BBC and in particular to its financing by a mandatory licence fee imposed on all owners of television sets in return for not accepting advertising revenue.

Mr. Murdoch, Iraq, and the Ukraine

Mr. Murdoch bears a heavy responsibility for the invasion of Iraq through his ownership at the time of the neo-conservatives' Weekly Standard which keeps them informed of the thinking of its leaders – led by that mastermind of the Iraq invasion, former US Vice President Dick Cheney. That is not all – Murdoch played a key role in the revival of the neo-conservatives who backed American tampering to establish that hegemonic Unipolar World – this time by making a new start by interfering in the Ukraine. So Murdoch is a link between Mrs. May and Article 50, the invasion of Iraq, the Ukrainian civil war and Putin's annexation of the Crimea.

And then of course Murdoch played a major role in securing the election of Donald Trump with his Fox News (most watched TV in the US) and his myriad press and radio holdings throughout the US. As in the UK he is now in at the top of the market with that much respected paper, the Wall Street Journal (he owns Dow Jones, the owners amongst many other things of the Journal), and going down market to tabloids, notably the highly successful New York Post with its profound influence on the opinions of average people. All this (I was told to fill my printer with ten sheets of A4 to print the full list of his assets throughout the world) created that alternative pro-Republican (or rather the more extreme 'Tea Party') mythical reality doing much to bamboozle the nearly 63 million who voted for Trump.

The weakened UK media enabling the leadership of Mr. Murdoch

Murdoch and Mrs. May were greatly helped by that curious phenomenon – the all-but universal unshakable conviction following the referendum, not just in the UK but worldwide, that the UK would 'inevitably' leave the EU which was becoming a self-fulfilling prophecy. The UK let down the United States - its true, non-Trump, vital national interest - the avoidance of Brexit to preserve the unity of the West. And the US media let down 'remain' in the months leading to May's invocation of Article 50 (29 March 2017) precisely because of this same unquestioning conviction that nothing could now stop Brexit. Notably the Washington Post, the New York Times, and CNN refused at the top editorial level to make an all out effort to explain that Brexit would be a disaster for the US as well as for the UK and the EU because of the – catastrophic may well be not too strong a word – damage it would do to Western unity already threatened by all four of those Brexiteers.

I myself was one of those who tried hard to persuade those responsible for editorial and opinion in all three of these without any success. One reason was their 'gatekeepers' would not let me in. Try contacting any of these and, unless you know the ropes, you will find how difficult it is to get a phone number that connects you to a human or an email address that actually arrives with the intended recipient.

The ideal of Europe and Pope Francis' speech accepting the Charlemagne prize, 2015

Here I believe I must first briefly digress once more to mention two obvious vulnerabilities of the European Union which have helped create the ambience in which 'leave' flourished. Consider just the problems of the Euro and of languages and it is easy to ignore the way Brexit causes us to forget the ideal of Europe. Yet many of us today, particularly those 'under 35s', recognise ourselves as Europeans as well as citizens of our own countries. And of course it is as Europeans that we are regarded when we travel outside - for example to China, the Middle East, Africa or even the United States.

It is this precious EU unity in a world often oblivious of pan European interests – EU west and Russian east - that is at present broken by the renewed separation from Russia, and since 29 March 2017 by the oncoming separation from the UK.

One person has reminded us of that ideal Europe, now even further away since Putin, a European, hacked the American election against Russia's true interests and Mrs. May's attempt to deny us our European identity. That is Argentinian Pope Francis. Here is a shortened version of his address with a one paragraph preface by a Catholic priest:

'Events all over Europe have marked the sixtieth anniversary of the signing of the Treaty of Rome and the triggering by Theresa May of Article 50 of the Lisbon treaty. So it is worth recalling the fullest exposition of Catholic teaching about Europe by the Holy Father, in a speech he made last May when he was awarded the *Charlemagne Prize*. It is best to let the Holy Father speak for himself in these extracts:

The ideal of Europe - Pope Francis on the occasion of his reception of the Charlemagne Prize in May 2015:

'They [the founders of Europe] were prepared to pursue alternative and innovative paths in a world scarred by war. Not only did they boldly conceive the idea of Europe, but they dared to change radically the models that had led only to violence and destruction. ...Today, in our own world, marked by so much conflict and suffering, there is a need to return to the same *de facto solidarity* and *concrete generosity* that followed the Second World War. The founding fathers were heralds of peace and prophets of the future. Today more than ever, their vision inspires us to build bridges and tear down walls...

The roots of our peoples, the roots of Europe, were consolidated down the centuries by the constant need to integrate in new syntheses the most varied and discrete cultures.

The identity of Europe is, and always has been, a dynamic and multicultural identity. Political activity cannot fail to see the urgency of this fundamental task. We know that "the whole is greater than the part, but it is also greater than the sum of the parts", and this requires that we work to "broaden our horizons and see the greater good which will benefit us all". We are asked to promote an integration that finds in solidarity a way of acting, a means of making history... If there is one word that we should never tire of repeating, it is this: dialogue.

We are called to promote a culture of dialogue by every possible means and thus to rebuild the fabric of society. The culture of dialogue entails a true apprenticeship and a discipline that enables us to view others as valid dialogue partners, to respect the foreigner, the immigrant and people from different cultures as worthy of being listened to. Today we urgently need to engage all the members of society in building "a culture which privileges dialogue as a form of encounter" and in creating "a means for building consensus and agreement while seeking the goal of a just, responsive and inclusive society...

I dream of a *new European humanism*... I dream of a Europe that is young, still capable of being a mother, a mother who has life because she respects life and offers hope for life... a Europe that cares for children, that offers fraternal help to the poor and those newcomers seeking acceptance because they have lost every-thing and need shelter...a Europe that is attentive to and concerned for the infirm and the elderly, lest they be simply set aside as useless... a Europe where being a migrant is not a crime but a summons to greater commitment on behalf of the dignity of every human being... a Europe where young people breathe the pure air of honesty, where they love the beauty of a culture and a simple life undefiled by the insatiable needs of consumerism, where getting married and having children is a responsibility and a great joy, not a problem due to the lack of stable employment...'

My comment on the Pope's ideal of Europe

Yes, Europe, East and West, has a single culture like a large sturdily built four-legged dining table on which more than 30 cultural offerings are laid out for consumption not only by the countries that contribute, but as a free gift to the entire world. That common culture has survived and thrives despite the history of crippling European wars and the political separation of Russia during the years of the USSR – and sadly, since the second Putin presidency.

.

The EU though, is like a tripod standing on three mutually supporting legs – Germany, France, and the UK. They balance and complement eachother - even as a triangle needs all three sides to exist. It was for lack of a UK leg at the beginning because of two vetoes by France's General de Gaulle that it had to be temporarily propped up willy-nilly. That led to serious errors – which it was hoped could be put right in the future. That prop was replaced with a true leg by the UK's accession in 1972. But that essential third leg now risks being torn off putting the entire ambitious EU experiment at risk. Nothing can replace that tripod so it will have to be seen whether a largely German-French EU would be able to attract sufficient support from other members to replace the UK and survive.

Here is the place to emphasise that the failure of the 'remain' campaign was compounded by its lamentable lack of imagination in failing to appeal to that ideal of Europe. That correct but dreary fixation during the 2016 referendum campaign with Brexit's economic disadvantages, should have been complemented with a positive and appealing note. We could have been reminded that the UK by its victories – however incomplete – in the two World Wars made possible the post war

Franco-German reconciliation expressed in the European Coal and Steel Community (ECSC) treaty in 1950, precursor to the European Economic Community which became the European Union. That forged an era of peace and mutual prosperity – the world's first experiment in mutual cooperation by previously hostile countries. Despite the flaws inevitable with any major international initiative, that reconciliation has succeeded in eliminating even the possibility of war for nearly 70 years. And that despite so bellicose a history brought unparalleled misery not just to Europe but to the entire world. It also reminded us of how the UK, despite a delayed start in actually joining the EU, was an indispensable partner in ensuring the firm foundations on which the whole edifice of the EU was built. What a romantic story appealing to young and old alike! Who would want to renounce being part of such a daring experiment and so put its very existence in doubt?

Of course the EU as an experiment in the making has many shortcomings notably that democratic deficit which has only now begun to be corrected.

Two EU shortcomings which deserve a mention: the Euro and languages

The Euro: Perhaps the most unfortunate error – it has brought a division in the EU – has proved to be the introduction of the **Euro** in 1999 where French desire to get something urgently needed for reforming the EU's defects, came up against German financial caution – a caution shared by the Bank of England. But Germany, still convalescing from the fall of the Berlin Wall and consequent re-unification in 1990, was still too weak to stand up to France's hurry for the Euro. So the Deutsche Bank, lacking the support of its equally prudent British counterpart the Bank of England was obliged to yield. The Euro proved a great success in oiling the daily purchases of the millions of individuals and businesses in the countries that use it. But on the other hand – in large part because of the 2007 US banking crisis - it has caused such serious problems as to be a factor threatening the

Union itself. It is ironic that Mr. Tony Blair – much maligned for undermining the EU by destabilising the Middle East as UK Prime Minister in 2003 - understood the imperative for a sound stable currency for the entire Union and sought to join the Germans in resisting the hurried attitude of the French.

Languages

Added to the financial vulnerability of the EU another vulnerability stems from the 23 official languages of the Union. Failure to take major action on language has worked against the idea of Europe and in favour of 'leave'. In 1963 Minister of State Edward Heath was working to achieve the UK's membership of the then European Economic Community to right Prime Minister Harold Macmillan's refusal in 1957 to add the UK to the then 6 members of the EEC and sign the Treaty of Rome (It was not until 1987 that the EEC became the EU under the 'Single European Act', 1987). So our Ambassador to France, Sir Pierson Dixon, asked me, then a First Secretary in his Embassy, to contact both the French and the British education ministries to propose a major joint action to ensure that in future there would be largest possible numbers of French and British fluent in both languages.

I found the French Education Ministry altogether enthusiastic and it prepared an aide memoire about the modalities of an exchange of French and English teachers so that French teachers in Britain and English teachers in France would be seconded for some years to the other country for this purpose. But the UK Ministry of Education pointed out that local authorities were responsible for state education in the UK and that there could be no assurance that teachers going to France would get their promotion or even be hired again by the same or even some other local authority.

There is little doubt that this would have changed had General de Gaulle not used his first veto against British membership of the EEC that same year, 1963. But the EEC/EU itself has failed since then to address the crying need for languages. Over the half-century since, many have decried the absence of a required language standard in the EU and that has been perhaps the main buffer to far greater integration and mutual understanding. For learning a country's language gives a student an insight into another culture while at the same time demonstrating the universality of the human condition. My own proposal was, and remains, that all children in the EU must demonstrate reasonable fluency in, as well as their own, at least one other of Europe's great languages – English, French, German, Italian, Spanish, and Russian.

Presidents Trump and Putin

Among the supporting documents, reports, speeches, and articles that make up the rest of this book, pages 96 to 138 deal with US President Trump and Russian President Putin and how they have revolutionised the international scene. Pp 138/40 describe President Putin's no-holds-barred campaign to ensure President Trump's election and to obtain a 'Leave' vote in the 2016 EU referendum in the UK, in both cases using Fancy Bear developed at least from 2002 – a cyber attack weapon with an algorythm which pinpoints where voting is likely to be particularly close, and hence where further attacks should be concentrated.

The world has only recently learned of (ex) Cambridge Analytica, a British company, whose founders were Steve Bannon, Trump's original Chief Strategist, and Robert Mercer financier who contributed $24m to Trump's campaign – he has a close relationship with Russian oligarch Dmitri Ribolev to whom Trump sold a Palm Beach mansion. Cambridge Analytica was notorious for its misuse of an immense amount of Facebook's data concerning over 50 million users – information which was used by Russian intelligence, in addition to Fancy Bear, to achieve Putin's ends in both the UK and in the US.

Everything points to Cambridge Analytica's intervention in both the Trump Election and the UK 'Brexit' referendum from June 2016 having largely relied on the expertise of Russian born Alexandr Kogan. He is both a Cambridge Lecturer and, on at least one occasion, a St. Petersburg Lecturer (in Russian) specialising in 'neuro-science and data' enabling cutting edge use of the information on 30 million Facebook users that he admits having harvested to influence voters. He denies any link with Russian intelligence but it is just such cyber work that Kogan does which is known to be particularly sought after by President Putin. There is therefore a very real possibility that with Cambridge Analytica and Fancy Bear – Putin was able to achieve his two top priority aims – Trump's election and the UK referendum 'Leave' vote. As people learn more about this, the UK electorate will likely insist that, with the very validity of the referendum in substantial doubt, its true will be confirmed either by a vote in parliament or by a second referendum.

Summary of the first part of this book

In these first 48 pages I have tried to make the argument against Brexit (in any form) showing how the mere prospect of Brexit has extremely dire implications for the UK's vital interests both internal and international. I have stressed how Britain playing its full role within the EU, is indispensable for ensuring that world's democracies avoid the very real prospect of the EU, now the bastion of democracy, unravelling. With the growth of populism the precedent of Brexit and American leadership of the West far from assured under the Trump presidency, that is a real possibility.

I have emphasised that the avoidance of Brexit requires a major shift in British opinion and how the American media has an essential role to play in 'shouting louder' – or rather more effectively - than the Murdoch led pro-Brexit UK media if the public is to be weaned from Prime Minister May's spurious 'patriotic' and 'democratic' Brexit and so have a far better opportunity to know the truth and its consequences.

The roles of the four Brexiteers are interdependent. All four, either consciously or unconsciously, are working towards President Putin's 'war by other means' to fracture the West and remove it as an obstacle to Russian pretensions. But when I have put this, even to Leave voters, all without exception want the UK to do everything it can to prevent such a global disaster.

To repeat: if Brexit is to be avoided public opinion will need to change markedly before a majority of MPs will <u>either</u> i) vote requiring the prime minister of the day to inform the EU Commission that the UK wishes to remain a member of the EU (see page 198 for the full text of Lord Kerr's lecture on Article 50 of 10 November 2017), <u>or</u> ii) for a second referendum arguing that a democracy has the right to change its mind, and that, on this occasion, must do so because of the many doubts about the fairness, even the validity of the 2016 referendum.

While politicians follow and in this case cannot outstrip the needed change in public opinion, every one else can openly argue to maximise the already fast growing opposition to Brexit. This is being shared by financiers (from Banks in City of London), by manufacturers (notably of cars), scientists (many reliant of EU funding for their British contribution to cutting edge work, notably on DNA), by NGOs with European and world activities, by the non-Brexit media – UK, EU, and US), and above all by a growing host of individuals among whom most importantly is the electorate.

So I have stressed from page 1 that young people, the key to change, need to be mobilised – by such as Femi Oluwole and Will Dry's Our Future Our Choice (OFOC) who are campaigning not only for young people to register to vote to save their future as Europeans, but to persuade the over 60s, whose 'Leave' votes ensured the 2016 referendum result, not just to think of themselves but of their children and grandchildren who don't want to be deprived for their lifetime of their heritage as Europeans.

As I have argued over and again those seeking to maximise the call to avoid Brexit must forcefully introduce into the Brexit argument the hitherto all but neglected subject of those dire international implications of Brexit, the mere prospect of which has already done immense damage to the unity of the West. Will Hutton and Andrew (Lord) Adonis, in their short book 'Saving Britain' have just made a compelling case for the UK to stay in the EU, reforming both itself and the EU, and so play its indispensable part in shoring up the EU – now threatening to unravel with the precedent of the UK's departure and the rise of populism. Their book and this one are complementary and should help spark the awareness of patriots – both 'remainers' and still 'leavers' - that Britain must not follow Trump's US into isolation. For Britain still has great power, no longer alone, but as maybe the most – internationally influential power in the EU. Britain is the one which could be most effective in preserving tue democracy and preventing arch Brexteer Putin (with a compliant Trump) from presiding over the fragmentation of the West.

It is not ewnough to go against Trump or Brexit: voters want a positive message giving hope. The Democrats in the US should take this to heart as well as Halt Brexiteers !

The irony is that both Trump (who has been confidently diagnosed by psychiatrists, although they have not examined the patient, as suffering from Narcissistic Personality Disorder – NPD, see Mayo clinic p. 222) - and Putin (highly gifted intelligence chief who has carried out the two most ambitious 'Special Political Actions', S.P.A., in history) have done immense harm to their own country's interests. As for Trump no one could have done more harm not just to himself but to the Presidency itself and to American relations with the world. Trump too, must not be allowed to succeed in fragmenting the West, now all-but entirely in the form of the EU. His decision to withdraw the US from the Iran deal (8 May) has brought home - even to some Brexiteers – that only the EU, crucially enjoying the weight of the UK, has the clout to contain Trump's threat to the global order – especially from his withdrawal decisions (Iran, Climate, trade agreeements etc.) – so preserve certainties in place of the uncertainties generated by his megalomnia. It is consistency of policy that makes it possible for the EU to work when required with Russia and China. With a monolithic EU the US can take time off to neutralise Trump.

Putin hoped to gain Trump's compliance and so would, on his terms, improve Russia's relations with the West – notably removing the sanctions that resulted from his annexation of the Ukraine. Instead both his operations have been 'blown' and Russian/US relations have scarcely been worse during most of the Cold War. Even his interference with the UK referendum is fast becoming known and the UK can now quite likely avoid Brexit in 2019 – both failures dashing his hopes of fracturing the West in his mistaken belief that this would maximise Russia's influence on the world stage. He failed his country by failing to see that the closest possible relations between the Russian east and the EU west of geographical Europe are essential if it is to hold the balance between a resurgent China and a no longer reliable America.

If Brexit is avoided and Putin's hopes for this second big gamble dashed, he will – already facing growing opposition even from his base – be open to EU calls to end his 'war by other means' if offered the opportunity to return to Peter the Great's insistence on Russia playing its due role in Europe. So, if UK opinion takes back the words 'democracy' and 'patriotism' usurped by 'Leave', the call to halt Brexit will not only be a call to make Brexit just yesterday's nightmare for so many people fearing the consequences for their jobs, but also an appeal to true patriotism: Britain giving the EU its indispensable support in defeating Putin's and Trump's attempts to fracture the West, so restoring a far better and more stable balance of power in the world.

===

Part two: reports, articles and speeches supporting the argument against Brexit made in these first 48 pages

i) THE FLAWED REFERENDUM AND ii) THE INTERNATIONAL IMPLICATIONS OF BREXIT

My first report on Brexit – the flawed referendum: 18 August 2016

SOME REASONS WHY THE CAMPAIGN LEADING UP TO THE 23 JUNE REFERENDUM RESULT WAS SEVERELY VITIATED AND THUS SHOULD NOT BE TAKEN AS REPRESENTING THE CONSIDERED VIEWS OF THE BRITISH PEOPLE.

The best round-up I have seen of the deeply flawed referendum campaign is John Lanchester's 'Brexit Blues' in the London Review of Books 28 July 2016. His conclusions are very similar to mine set out here.

The requirement for a referendum if it is to reflect the true will of the electorate

If a referendum is to reflect the reasonably well informed will of the voters there must be easy access to the basic facts needed to make a decision. This was not the case with the UK's 23 June referendum, and considering the controversy that had come to surround the subject, the UK's EU membership was not a suitable subject for a referendum. To make an informed judgment in these circumstances one needed some knowledge of economics, foreign affairs, and sociology.

Voters usually vote with some strongly held belief. This generally works quite well when voting for a Member of Parliament who then becomes responsible for taking decisions on behalf of his constituents as they arise in the Commons where emotion is commonly balanced by reason. But emotional elements – e.g. the protest element, the patriotic element – can readily determine the outcome of a referendum without due regard to the question asked.

I am concerned here to show prima facie that the 23 June referendum was so deeply flawed that it should not be accepted as the considered will of those who voted – let alone of those who either could not, or chose not to vote.

The history of the referendum on UK membership of the EU
Because of the rapid rise of Nigel Farage's UKIP (UK Independence Party) demanding that the UK leave the EU, and increased euroscepticism in the Conservative Party including among many of its MPs, its leader David Cameron undertook in 2013 to hold a referendum on UK membership of the EU before the end of 2017 if the Conservatives came to power in the 2015 elections. They did with a small overall majority. Cameron's aim was thus to overcome the damaging division among Conservatives over the EU with a 'Yes' vote.

When his gamble failed a considerable number of Conservative MPs – both 'Yes' and 'No' begged Cameron to remain until the autumn to allow a period of calm reflection before deciding on the way ahead. He ignored this appeal and resigned precipitately thereby likely doing more damage to the UK than he had done even by the way he had conducted the referendum itself. For that enabled Theresa May abruptly to succeed him as Prime Minister and, though ostensibly his supporter for 'Yes', straightway declared that she is in fact a convinced Brexiter and 'Brexit means Brexit'. So it is precisely those anti-EU

Conservatives whom Cameron had planned to subdue, who now govern the UK.

Possibly more than by anything else, Cameron's defeat can be explained by his decision to allow Ministers in his government freedom to campaign for 'No' while yet remaining in office. That caused much confusion. This was his referendum and it required his leadership and not contradiction from within his own government. In addition he failed to prepare the electorate for the referendum - instead, rather than choosing some date in 2017, he put it forward to June 2016. Then, as the possibility of a 'No' majority increased, apparently in desperation, he ran his own campaign ever less astutely.

Widespread Ignorance that this was an advisory referendum
The most striking thing about the referendum - both in the UK and abroad - is the almost universal acceptance that the comparatively small majority of votes for 'No' means that the UK is now obliged to leave the EU. The result was 48%-52%, a majority of 1.2m out of 33.5m votes cast – certainly not a clear decision, rather proof of a country divided in half which demanded of any government the most careful consideration of the best interests of the UK before deciding on any action. Had all UK passport holders resident outside the UK – those most affected by the result - had the vote 'yes' would certainly have won. And if even just the 1.2m UK residents in the EU all had the vote the 'no' majority would have been much diminished.

This result also ignores those in the UK who did not vote, or even register – for example the young who feel estranged from today's political class, and Labour voters who could not bring themselves to an unpopular Conservative Prime Minister's unnecessary referendum.

The young, the so-called millennials, who did vote voted massively for 'remain'. They were aware that their future, more than that of any other group, was at stake: European by birth they would have to live far longer in the confines of 'little England' than the middle aged who voted 'no'. But so many of the under 25s did not trouble to register, feeling that they have little in common with today's political scene. It is worth mentioning them again further on.

Yet this was a purely <u>Advisory Referendum</u> and the result is not in fact binding on any Prime Minister or Government (although former Prime Minister Cameron did say that he personally would accept the result). Even a great many 'Yes' voters believe that they must swallow objections, no matter how profound, because the 'British people have spoken' and so an extreme interpretation of 'democracy' must be allowed to prevail. Indeed, at the end of July, it seems almost taboo to talk of avoiding Brexit for fear of provoking 'Leave' voters – although many of these are known to be having second thoughts. And surely the UK's national interest should come before concerns about the reaction of some 'Leave' voters – even if they number some in the present government.

The flaws in the referendum campaign
The campaign was dominated by misrepresentation by 'Leave' and incompetence by 'Remain'.

This February I went to the UK to assess the situation in the four month lead up to the referendum. Since then I have done what I can to support the 'remain' campaign both through personal contacts and organisations - notably Lord Rose's 'Britain Stronger In Europe' and Alan Johnson MP's 'Labour In for Britain'.

During my enquiries in the UK, like so many others, I soon came to the conclusion that the whole campaign was deeply flawed by that misrepresentation and incompetence.

<u>Misrepresentation by 'Leave'</u>
Misrepresentation, even outright untruths, by the leaders - Messrs. Boris Johnson MP, Michael Gove MP, and Nigel Farage leader of UKIP, is well documented. Statistics about the cost of the EU to the UK were so often incorrect that the Statistics Authority complained at their misuse. In addition so much was suppressed. Here I only mention the claim that the UK pays £8bn annually to the EU – without mentioning that in subsidies and other payments it gets some £4bn back - and the famous Boris Johnson campaign bus with its claim in huge letters 'We send the EU £350m a week let's fund our NHS instead' when in fact the figure is less than half that.

Boris Johnson declared more than once that the referendum provided a 'once in a lifetime … opportunity to take back control of our country' – an emotive phrase that ignored the fact that every treaty a country signs involves some loss of sovereignty, some lack of that 'control'. Free trade agreements inevitably involve a marked loss of sovereignty – and so would any arrangement the UK negotiated with the EU following Brexit. In a word, no attempt was made by 'leave' correctly to inform voters about what to expect from Brexit. On the contrary, 'leave' consistently played down the years of uncertainty that would necessarily follow, giving voters the impression that whatever they wanted from a 'No' vote would be realised, if not immediately, then after only a short delay. Here are just two typical remarks illustrating the confusion about the referendum: in Peterborough a worker complained after voting 'No' – 'When are those Pakis leaving ' – failing to realise that only immigration from the EU would be limited by Brexit, not the presence of those from the Indian subcontinent whose immigration is under entirely UK control. And in Bournemouth a middle aged accountant with a degree in the subject remarked 'why vote? They always come back until they get the answer they want' (as in the case of the Irish referendums) not understanding the different nature of this advisory referendum.

'Leave' – and notably Boris Johnson - campaigned on the proposition that they knew better than the UK, EU and foreign politicians and experts – including Barack Obama and the Canadian Governor of the Bank of England - who strongly advised that UK remain in the EU. But when 'No' prevailed, many were shocked to learn that none of the 'leave' leaders had any plan for arriving at 'Brexit' – indeed Boris Johnson found it politic to disappear from the scene. Their campaign had largely appealed to populist sentiment, not to persuasion with facts. And such populism is currently also threatening democracy in the US (Donald Trump), France (Marine Le Pen), and in a number of other countries.

Another serious misrepresentation – so flagrant as to be termed an outright lie by some observers – was 'leave' leaders' claim that after Brexit the UK, being so important to the EU, would have access to the Common Market without accepting free movement of EU citizens. This despite clear warnings from EU leaders who fear the EU itself could unravel if the UK left and got any such deal (some other countries might well want the same). Any lingering hopes of such an outcome were dashed on 27 July when the President of the Commission, Jean-Claude Juncker, named the hardline EU operative Michel Barnier as the EU's chief negotiator for Brexit.

The media's bias towards 'Leave'
Much of the media – struggling against competition from the internet - gave 'leave's most dubious statements headline coverage in search of circulation at the expense of accuracy. Notably, the Daily Telegraph favoured Brexit, continuing to feature their lead correspondent, Boris Johnson, elaborating on his habitual contempt for the EU, where he had first made his name as the Telegraph's correspondent in Brussels.

Rupert Murdoch, the American, former Australian, the world's leading purveyor of news, also favoured Brexit. His 'The Sun' the UK's highest circulation tabloid (1.8 million) did at least as much damage to 'remain': two examples - Murdoch associate Michael Gove was involved in getting The Sun's front page 'The Queen Backs Brexit' headline plus full page photo. Although the piece was found 'substantially misleading', the damage to 'remain' must have been considerable given the all but universal popularity of the Queen. Many in the rest of the media made much of it.

On 22 June readers woke up to The Sun's headline 'BeLEAVE in Britain'. This after hearing Boris Johnson's dramatic appeal the night before 'Make the 23rd of June Britain's Independence Day' - the closing words of the BBC's 'Great Debate' which in fact was not a debate which would have given an opportunity for Yes' to set out its basic case. It was in fact a major two hour questions programme which favoured 'leave' with its penchant for short slogans. So even the well-trusted and supposedly impartial BBC finally came down for 'No'.

Even more importantly, Boris Johnson, more of a self-publicising journalist than a politician, became the TV personality of the campaign, generally without corrective reporting. Without any need for bias by TV stations, through constant exposure Boris Johnson became the TV star throughout - the referendum celebrity when it is celebrities who are revered, not politicians. Johnson made light of the problems that Britain would face if it were to leave the EU and of the long period of delay and uncertainty that would necessarily follow. Indeed, when 'No' got a majority, Boris Johnson had no plan for 'Brexit' and faded into obscurity until appointed Foreign Secretary by Theresa May, Cameron's successor who had been for 'In', but overnight became a Prime Minister doggedly resolved to lead the UK to Brexit. The then German Foreign Minister spoke for many when he described Johnson's appointment in one word: 'ungeheurlich' - outrageous.

Exposure on TV not only ensures that you are known, but that your message, however extreme, is unforgettable. Frequent appearance on TV does much to magnify the spread of populism in the US (Donald Trump), France (Marine Le Pen) and the UK (Boris Johnson) where extreme statements which resonate with certain elements of the population are believed with little question.

Incompetence of 'Remain'

Misrepresentation by 'Leave' and the bias of much of the media made it difficult enough to find factual information about the key issues raised by the referendum. But this was compounded by the incompetence of 'Remain'. Both Lord Stuart Rose's 'Britain Stronger In Europe' and Alan Johnson's 'Labour In for Britain' failed lamentably in getting across their essential message to the general public and to former Labour voters in particular. When 'Britain Stronger In' was founded on 12 October 2015, much of the media predicted failure. Lord Rose, a businessman, lacked the needed political savvy and was prone to making unfortunate remarks - even forgetting the name of the organisation of which he was Chair. He kept a low profile and in any case was very far from the charismatic TV personality needed to oppose Boris Johnson that 'Stronger In' so urgently needed. Indeed the failure to find one was a major reason for the failure of 'Stronger In'. It is surprising that such a second rate organisation became the 'official' spokesman for 'Yes' on 13 April 2016. If the body politic had bothered, the UK could have set up a far more effective body for such an extremely important purpose.

i) 'Britain Stronger In Europe'

'Stronger In' concentrated, efficiently enough, on the economic advantages of staying in the EU but ignored the fact that referendum voters are less interested in dry facts than their need to feel a strong emotional incentive for their decision - something that touches them personally. 'Leave' though, skillfully sounded a chord with its emphasis on immigration and patriotism – two key issues 'Stronger In' largely ignored these even though they was expressly drawn to its attention. But even if it had been more responsive and had heeded advice, it lacked the means and publicity savoir faire to put this across to the public – something all but impossible without that TV personality.

ii) 'Labour In For Britain'

When, in October 2015, I was first in touch with Alan Johnson – the MP charged with Labour's campaign for a 'Yes' vote through 'Labour In For Britain' - he appeared to be well informed of the problems and likely to conduct an effective campaign. But in the event his 'Labour In For Britain' was even more of a disappointment than 'Stronger In'. Its website was the same day after day and there was no contact given so I was unable to get the text of Jeremy Corbyn's speech of 14 April 2016, one of, if not the, best speeches for 'Yes'. (I got my copy through the party's regular website 'Labour List').

Indeed this exceptional speech was almost entirely overlooked by the media which had long been disparaging Corbyn whatever he said. Almost alone, the speech made much of the important role Britain had in the reform of the EU, desired by so many of both its countries and peoples, to make the EU more responsive to its peoples and less of a club for capitalists. That countered a key 'leave' assertion that the EU is incapable or reform.

Corbyn, one of the few who looked beyond Britain to the wider world, pointed out that it was the EU that guaranteed many of the human and other rights of workers. He put Climate Change deservedly first in his list of challenges which the EU countries – with Britain - could only resolve together. As he put it – 'It is not the EU that is the problem but a Conservative Government ....' This speech deserves reading today as an example of how the media – and Labour itself – ignored the truly important issues for voters. Despite comments that Mr. Corbyn felt obliged to say what he did and that he was only too happy to abandon

'Yes' when the 'No' vote prevailed, I have appended this speech at the end of this book – it got very little publicity and failed to encourage 'Yes' voting as it should have.

The Labour Party shares a heavy responsibility for the incompetence of 'remain' which left 'leave' to be positive and strike the note of hope so important in attracting voters. Indeed, examining the results throughout the UK, Labour may well have lost the referendum. It utterly failed to persuade its traditional supporters that – as its Leader Jeremy Corbyn had stressed so persuasively – a 'yes' vote was greatly in their interest. 'Yes' would be a Labour win – not just a Cameron Conservative win, while a 'No' would be a licence for the most diehard Tories to run the country at the expense of the working man and of the UK itself.

But Labour did not recover in time from the unexpected collapse of its vote in the 2015 election. Despite the election of Jeremy Corbyn as its left wing Leader, Labour had not learned the lesson of its failure to meet the aspirations, concerns, and bitterness of its traditional voters mainly from the white working class. Tony Blair's New Labour under David Miliband was too much of a left-of-centre form of the Conservative party to be capable of exploiting the disillusion and anger caused by those dire effects of globalization on traditional ways of life. One of the most painful of these being so called 'zero hour contracts' removing security of employment from as many as 1m British workers and affecting many more. This too, had little to do with the EU, rather it reflected the misdirected policies of David Cameron's government. In the absence the traditional loyalty to Labour, this exasperation expressed itself in a massive protest vote against EU membership.

This protest vote was also fuelled by immigration – whole towns had become socially unrecognisable not only as a result of immigration mainly from the Indian sub-continent (under UK government control) but also because of immigrants from the EU – notably from its poorer countries (due to the EU requirement for free movement of its citizens over which individual countries had no control). These two were frequently confused.

On this immensely important issue, not only Labour and 'Stronger In' but Cameron himself suffered a major setback when the latest figure for 330,000 net arrivals from the EU was published shortly before the vote. This setback was unnecessary. It resulted from the incompetence not only of 'Remain' but of Cameron himself – for the figure included 169,000 students so only 161,000 could be classed as immigrants (barely above the 140,000 considered not only acceptable but desirable). The misleading 330,000 figure did Cameron and the case for 'Remain' great harm because immigration had by then become the leading issue for so many voters.

iii) <u>Patriotism</u> - this deserves separate mention for to some extent it influences all voters. I have already mentioned the damage done to 'Remain' by The Sun's front page headline 'The Queen backs Brexit' with its misleading message for patriots.

Appealing to patriotism was a staple ploy for 'leave', but surprisingly barely featured in 'remain' publicity. Here again 'Stronger In' ignored advice to challenge 'leave' on this emotional issue.

'Leave' painted a picture of a Britain of the past, all but entirely white, and with the worldwide respect due to a country, once the possessor of the world's greatest empire, and the 'winner' of both World Wars. The image was of everyone standing together as Britain stood alone during its Finest Hour.

'Remain' failed to use TV to put across the up-to-date, forward looking, alternative which had been suggested and is worth sketching here. It told of how England and later Britain, for more than four centuries had fought wars at great expense in blood and treasure to prevent any power dominating Europe - from Spain's Philip II, France's Louis XIV and Napoleon, to Germany's Kaiser and Hitler. And after that Britain had played a major role in countering the pretensions of the Soviet Union. Throughout this history Britain had prevailed thanks to allies - so it was with European allies that Britain had at last done so much to establish the period of peace after World War II that made possible the great experiment of a European Union of all its peoples and dominated by none.

Did voters really want the UK now to turn its back on friends and partners leaving them in the lurch at a time of crisis when UK support was sorely needed? And did 'leave' voters really want to leave to a reluctant Germany the leadership of the EU?

This appeal to patriotism would have appealed to many, and in particular to the elderly who, in the event, voted massively for 'leave'.

Labour too, failed to publicise the rather different patriotism implied in Corbyn's 14 April speech – the solidarity of all workers 'by hand or brain'. Here the emphasis was on the great role for Britain in leading the much desired reform of the EU – as I have said, to make the Union more in the interest of its peoples, and less of a purely economic vehicle for business and finance. And, as importantly, here was the opportunity with its partners in the EU for Britain to take a lead in facing up to the great challenges of Climate Change, emigration, Russia, and the prevention of terrorism - all beyond the UK's powers to deal with alone.

One observer aptly noted: 'If the UK puts as much effort into reforming the EU as it would have to in order to make a success of Brexit, the UK and the EU would both be better off'.

Neglect of the 'millenials'

Just as Labour failed so dismally to understand the extent of the grievances of its usual supporters, so all those working for 'Yes' equally failed to gain the votes of the 'millenials' already mentioned. There was no imagination, no enthusiasm to reach out to the idealism of the under 25s – involving their celebrities, using their music, and addressing their feelings of disinterest and isolation from the humdrum materialism of the world of the over 35s around them. Yet such an approach would have got many more to register and many more actually to vote in order to preserve their influence and ensure their participation in making the Europe of the future and its clout in the world. Votes enough at least further to dent that million and quarter majority for 'Leave'.

Threat to the UK as at present constituted

Scotland voted to remain, so did Northern Ireland. This raises complex questions about a) the ability of Scotland to leave the UK in order to remain in the EU, or to remain in the UK but retain membership of the EU, and b) the legislation that would be needed to avoid the return of the border between Northern Ireland and the Irish Republic – a border that would in fact become a frontier between the UK and the EU. It appears that all parties in the North, whatever their other differences, are anxious to avoid that. The obvious and probably the only solution would be to exclude Northern Ireland from Brexit if a return to 'the troubles' is to be avoided.

Leave played down the threat to the UK's integrity and 'remain', typically did not explain just how difficult these issues would be to resolve in the event of a 'No' vote, nor the possibility that, after 'No', Scotland might actually leave the Union despite the result of the 2014 referendum.

If 'remain' had made more of these issues, quite a few votes could have been different.

Few voting in a referendum – or even in an election – are much swayed by foreign policy. There was quite a bit said about the diminution of Britain's influence in the world if alone rather than acting through the EU. Just one example that was hardly mentioned was Hong Kong, perpetually under pressure from the government in Peking. Here the UK, acting discreetly with the EU, has had significant influence in helping preserve Hong Kong's quasi-independent status. Without the importance the EU has for Peking, the intervention of Britain alone could more easily be dismissed as unacceptable from the previous colonial power.

And Gibraltar must to be forgotten. With the UK in the European Union along with Spain, there is no case for the return of Gibraltar. With Brexit Spain is likely to renew this claim despite the wishes of the Gibraltarians.

A final word
I conclude this note by drawing attention to way the world goes on as usual after the shock of the British referendum. The international media has moved on to other news simply accepting that the UK will now be too busy with the highly complex and long term self-inflicted problem of leaving the EU to be able to play the part it should in the world. There are observers in the UK, in the EU, and in the world who still ask how Brexiters and their new Prime Minister, against the advice of the UK's friends and allies and with that mere 52% v. 48%, majority, can possibly go for Brexit with such self-assurance and determination when, even with all possible optimism, any possible advantages of leaving the UK would be negligible compared with those of 'remaining'.

Here in France, where British common sense has long been cited with some envy, observers find it hard to believe that the least informed are tugging the better informed into an unknown and dubious future letting the distraction of Brexit prevent the UK from dealing with the world's great problems with its allies as its importance requires.

I much hope that this offering, and no doubt others similar, will help towards making the case that only Parliament can take the decision to trigger Article 50 of the Lisbon Treaty. Surely no one person, let alone such a single-minded and determined a Brexiter as Prime Minister May, can be left to take Britain out of the European Union on the basis of a referendum so deeply flawed as even this short note has shown? I hope that those far better qualified than I, will put together the readily available information and present properly drawn up evidence of the unacceptability of the referendum result both for the Courts this October, and for the public. (Article 50 attached, followed by Article 49).

Article 50

1. Any Member State may decide to withdraw from the Union in accordance with its own constitutional requirements.

2. A Member State which decides to withdraw shall notify the European Council of its intention. In the light of the guidelines provided by the European Council, the Union shall negotiate and conclude an agreement with that State, setting out the arrangements for its withdrawal, taking account of the framework for its future relationship with the Union. That agreement shall be negotiated in accordance with Article 218(3) of the Treaty on the Functioning of the European Union. It shall be concluded on behalf of the Union by the Council, acting by a qualified majority, after obtaining the consent of the European Parliament.

3. The Treaties shall cease to apply to the State in question from the date of entry into force of the withdrawal agreement or, failing that, two years after the notification referred to in paragraph 2, unless the

European Council, in agreement with the Member State concerned, unanimously decides to extend this period.

4. For the purposes of paragraphs 2 and 3, the member of the European Council or of the Council representing the withdrawing Member State shall not participate in the discussions of the European Council or Council or in decisions concerning it.

A qualified majority shall be defined in accordance with Article 238(3)(b) of the Treaty on the Functioning of the European Union.

5. If a State which has withdrawn from the Union asks to rejoin, its request shall be subject to the procedure referred to in Article 49.

University College London Constitution Unit note:

The first point to note about Article 50 is that it is a once-and-for-all decision; there is no turning back once Article 50 has been invoked. If no acceptable *withdrawal* agreement has been reached after two years, the exiting Member State is left without any deal with the EU. It is of course possible to extend the time period. But this is in the gift of the EU Council and requires its unanimous agreement.

Article 49. Any European State which respects the values referred to in **Article** 2 and is committed to promoting them may apply to become a member of the Union. The European Parliament and national Parliaments shall be notified of this application. [A way back!]

Here is my second report on Brexit of 16 December 2016 about the international implications of Brexit:

UK must avoid Brexit and not quit the EU in this Hour of Maximum Danger: Trump, populism, refugees demand UK action to strengthen EU & the West

The need for opposition: Labour's opportunity

Arriving in Britain 6 months after the referendum for the High Court hearings in December was 'culture shock'. To my amazement, the implications of any sort of Brexit for the UK's foreign policy - Britain's place in the world - are barely mentioned. And this at a time when the future of the EU and of the 'West' is at stake and polls suggest that some 75% of Britons want the UK to play its full part on the world scene. Yet none seem aware that any form of Brexit would weaken the EU and the 'West' although the UK's prime national interest is to ensure that they are strengthened. This contradiction goes unnoticed - no one was even talking of avoiding Brexit let alone organising a campaign for continued EU membership.

Much confusion even about an advisory referendum

Instead, on this my first visit since the 23 June referendum, I found a country in thrall to 'leave' as populist Prime Minister Mrs. May leads the country to Brexit with steely determination. And this with most of the media applauding Brexit, mistrusted politicians in a quandary, widespread fear of 'leavers', and a public resigned to its fate bemused by endless arguments about 'hard' or 'soft' Brexit. But of course what the UK gets is in the gift of an unhelpful European Commission with the approval of the European Court of Justice. Most surprising of all was the persisting ignorance about the requirements of an advisory referendum – as this one was. There is of course no obligation to give effect to the majority vote. On the contrary, government has solely to consider the referendum campaign and then act in the best interests of the UK.

On the continent much concern at defection of the UK

In contrast, in France (where I live), Germany, and Italy there is a pervading sense of crisis: nationalist populism – Trump in the US, Mrs. May in the UK, Marine Le Pen in France, and neo-nationalists even in Germany - all threatening the solidarity of the West. It is not only well-informed contacts in the EU countries and in others like the US, who are alarmed. Our French plumber was typical when he asked with some bitterness how 'les Anglais', loyal allies whom the French once envied for their common sense, could possibly desert their EU partners at such a critical time with Trump in the wings.

Trump's extreme uncertainty and the EU

For Donald Trump, even before taking office on January 20, has already brought extreme uncertainty to the world with his choice of advisers, his proposed Cabinet members, and with his disturbing contradictory 'tweets' about world affairs, impervious to expert advice – notably on NATO and President Putin's Russia. Exxon's erstwhile boss Rex Tillerson the UK is hardly less qualified to be US Secretary of State than Boris Johnson is to be UK Foreign Secretary – and his appointment led German Foreign Minister Frank-Walter Steinmeyer to make exclaim 'ungeheurlich' - outrageous. Like the morale in the State Department, it is no wonder that morale in the UK Diplomatic Service has received a severe jolt.

Ever since World War II the West has sheltered under an American umbrella. Now Europe has to accept that it must summon its own strength to face up to populism, be responsible for its own security, and pursue its own vital interests irrespective of the US – with Russia first on the agenda.

Putin's war by other means is against EU as well as US democracy

At least since 2007, when Fancy Bear hacker was first detected, Putin's Russia has been effectively at war with the 'West' – EU as well as US - using 'Special Political Action' (intelligence services seeking political ends) to unprecedented effect: cyber attacks coupled with false information spread through social media and subverting individuals with concealed payments. Edward Lucas' 'Spies, Lies, and How Russia Dupes The West' was published in 2012 (prompting Russia to be dubbed a 'katascopic state' – kataskopos = spy). Putin's 'interference' with democracy uses all arms of the state including the disposition of armed forces to alarm and undermine morale.

Russian and FBI intervention can be considered decisive

There is now no real doubt that by far the most successful SPA operation in history was ex-KGB Putin's success in securing the election of Donald Trump as 45th U.S. president with the help of FBI chief James Comey (who will have known of Russian intervention when he too, intervened). Paul Krugman, NYT 12 Dec. 2016, shows that Mrs. Clinton lost Michigan, Wisconsin and Pennsylvania by less than 1% and Florida by only a little more yet if any three of these states had gone for Clinton she would be president. It is all-but inconceivable that Putin and Comey's interventions did not alter the vote by more than 1%.

It is significant that it is the GRU, the Russian military intelligence service, that is responsible for the coordination of the role of the armed forces with the actions of the intelligence services. Military power, which demands respect and creates fears, works in concert with the covert work of the intelligence services – together they achieve the political results that Putin's government seeks. Putin's uncooperative military action in Syria is part of this 'war' against the West for the aggrandisement of Russia. It is important to recognise that Putin's war by other means is far from confined to the US. He has already had major successes promoting populist-nationalism in the EU. It is likely that high on his agenda are the German and French elections this year (there are suggestions, not confined to those made by Ben Bradshaw MP in the House of Commons, that Putin's attacks on EU democracy may have begun with the use of highly sophisticated algorithms during the UK's referendum campaign, targeting specific constituencies to enhance the 'no' vote).

Trump an unlikely Putin puppet

So Donald Trump will be 'the Russian president' (remember 'The Manchurian Candidate' ?) while Russia wages cyber war against the US. But this does not mean that he will necessarily seek a 'reset' for US Russia relations harmful to the US. Indeed Putin is likely to find the 45th President far from the puppet he would like. He too, could find Trump's policies impossible to discern for, an ignoramus in foreign affairs, Trump is capable of tweeting one thing and its opposite the same day. He enjoys keeping the world on tenterhooks. Trump's one constant is what Trump believes is good for Trump and his family – not what is in the best interests of the US, though these may at times coincide.

Putin's popularity over the Ukraine – it is also his Achilles heel
Putin, like Trump and Mrs. May, is a nationalist populist – he won his popularity by opposing the not so secret neo-conservative intervention in the Ukraine in 2014, a part of their SPA attempt to create a US unipolar world ignoring EU interests. Remember neo-con US Assistant Secretary of State Victoria Nuland, and her 'F... the Europeans?' Here the State Department cooperated with the neo-cons in the CIA in an attempt to make the Ukraine a pawn in the creation of that 'unipolar' world long sought by the neo-cons led by Vice President Dick Cheney and the PNAC (Project for a New American Century). Perhaps Mrs. Clinton's two worst mistakes were that vote for the invasion of Iraq which led to the destabilization of the Middle East and half our troubles today, and for permitting, albeit unwittingly, the comeback of the neo-conservatives after they had been forced to lie low after Obama's election.

For all Russians, the Ukraine is a vital interest for security and historic reasons – Kiev is the home of Russia. But Putin's bellicose foreign policy – of which he is so proud - using both Russia's armed forces and his cyber war against the West is in fact contrary to the prime national interest of Russia. As most Russians well know that is to have the closest possible relations with the EU in order to give Europe in its entirety far greater clout on the world stage – now even more essential with the advent of Trump. This is Putin's Achilles heel: it would be hard for him to oppose a well publicised EU offer of such a partnership provided Russia ceases to confront the West, coupled with a simultaneous offer to work out a plan to respect that Russian special interest in the Ukraine. We must not believe Russian polls vaunting Putin's 'immense' popularity – he makes sure they do.

The greatest danger to the UK, the EU, and the West: the conviction that Brexit is inevitable

So both Putin and Trump are presenting existential threats to the EU and the 'West'. Obviously the UK must not desert its friends and allies. But in the UK that mantra is ubiquitous: 'the British people have spoken and they want to quit the EU'. So it is unquestioned that 'to go against the people's will is to flout democracy' regardless of the fact that it is daily becoming more evident that breaking with the EU is immensely complicated and will absorb UK attention for years to come; and the fact that the entire world is in crisis and needs the strongest possible Europe. Clearly Britain's first task is to prevent the EU unravelling because of a selfish quest for Brexit. And that includes united action to counter Putin's current efforts to subvert EU democracy.

Avoiding Brexit is not 'flouting democracy': the vote not the 'clear will' of the British people

But how is it that there is this astonishing conviction that Brexit is inevitable and that 'leave' voters should be pandered to while 'remain' voters are not just ignored but heaped with obloquy although the electorate was all-but divided in half: 51.89% for 'leave' and 48.11% for 'remain'? This is without taking into account the 5 million odd UK overseas passport holders – the ones most affected by 'leave' – who had no vote. Indeed the Economist's Data Unit found that towards the end of 2016 more 'leave' than 'remain' voters regretted their choice – enough to sway opinion in favour of 'remain'. And this is also without taking into account either the many Labour sympathisers who could not bring themselves to vote for 'Cameron's Tories', or the 'millenials', disenchanted with boring middle-aged politicians, who often did not even register to vote but who are now awakening to the theft of their future as Europeans.

The severely flawed campaign

Then, profoundly affecting the outcome, was the campaign itself which was marked by deliberate misrepresentations by 'leave' – who notably failed to warn of the inevitably long drawn out daunting complications of leaving the EU – and the striking incompetence of 'remain': both the obscure Lord Rose's campaign 'Britain Stronger In Europe' run by Will Straw, and by 'Labour In for Britain' run by Alan Johnson. Much has been published about these serious defects which are perhaps best summed up in John Lanchester's 'Brexit Blues' in the July edition of the London Review of Books. My own, very similar, First Report on Brexit of 18 August 2016 is at dipconsult.blogspot.fr.

Two incidents stand out – leading Brexiter Michael Gove claiming, without evidence, that the Queen favoured Brexit. This was particularly damaging to 'remain' given the Queen's popularity among most of the population. And the BBC permitting its widely viewed 'Great Debate' on the eve of the referendum to close with Boris Johnson, the chief personality for 'leave,' with his emotional appeal 'make June 23 Britain's independence day'. This was followed next morning by arch-Brexiteer American Rupert Murdoch's full page headlines in his top circulation Sun: 'We urge our readers to beLEAVE in Britain'.

Indeed 'remain' was much hampered throughout the campaign and still is by much of the UK press taking its lead from Murdoch. The Daily Telegraph, the most influential quality paper, vigorously supported Brexit and still does: its lead EU correspondent Boris Johnson, like

Trump in the US, was the key TV campaigner getting massive free publicity for their populist aims.

As early as February 2016 many observers, myself included, warned both 'remain' campaigns that they were concentrating on dull economic arguments for staying in the EU while neglecting the powerful anti-EU feelings of so many far from Whitehall that successive governments – both Labour and Conservative - had overlooked. As in the US (and this got us Trump), too many in the UK have been left behind by globalisation, impoverished by the 2007 banking collapse, and forced to take 'zero hour contracts'. And few things are worse than daily fear of losing your job. On top of this is that widespread resentment at EU immigrants competing with Britons for limited social services and NHS resources. In the US it was 'keep America white', in the UK it was keep Britain British.

But it is not the EU but successive UK governments, Conservative and Labour, that, mostly in the name of a misguided 'austerity', ignored this - losing touch with their voters and forfeiting their loyalty. It seems that sufficient 'leave' voters blamed the EU for many of Whitehall's faults to explain 'leave's' close referendum result.

For all these reasons, Mrs. May never did, and does not now, express the 'clear will of the British People'. And that is without considering the wishes of Scotland and Northern Ireland.

Avoiding Brexit, the difficulties

So what can be done to prevent this determined lady and the small clique around her, in defiance of that ever-increasing evidence, resolutely invoking Article 50 and thus irrevocably setting the UK on the road to Brexit? And dragging the UK into years of painful all-absorbing negotiations to separate the UK from the EU, thereby sacrificing Britain's vital interests in the world for the nebulous, never honestly described advantages of Brexit?

On the face of it there is no problem. If, as expected around 12 January 2017, the UK Supreme Court demands formal parliamentary approval before Article 50 can be invoked, all that is required is for the more than 470 MPs of all parties out of a total of 650 to vote as they did in the referendum for 'remain' and thus against such invocation. But, in a snap non-binding vote called by Mrs. May on 8 December while the High Court was still sitting, 448 MPs voted in favour of invoking Article 50 with only 75 against. These are the only MPs to have voted unequivocally against Brexit. There is much fear of a backlash from disgruntled 'leavers' – Gina Miller, the lead litigant contesting Mrs. May's claim to invoke Article 50 on her own, has police guard after receiving death threats. Other lawyers and their principals have been browbeaten. I myself found 'leavers' will not argue in what was once the British way, but angrily condemn you for being unpatriotic, undemocratic and spurning that 'will of the people'.

Why could parliament vote to end its own supremacy?

Like every one, 'remain' MPs are aware of this intimidation. And those from majority 'leave' constituencies fear losing their seats so some are ready to sacrifice Britain's interests. This partly explains how MPs could actually vote to end by Act of Parliament the UK remaining a parliamentary democracy as the High Court has ruled that it is! Without parliament's supremacy Prime Ministers could enforce populist measures against parliament's wishes. Yet all this anxiety is unfounded – just as parliament can refuse to pass an Act authorising the invocation of Article 50, so it can refuse permission for Mrs. May to call an early election under the Fixed Term Parliaments Act, 2011.

A crippling lack of information

All this also reflects that all-but total lack of information about what is at stake internationally. Many, even MPs, are calling for a second referendum once the terms Mrs. May gets from the EU are known. This is mistaken for, whatever she may say, these will not be known before she invokes Article 50, and after that, when what is on offer becomes clearer, it would be too late.

This lack of information is due to that conviction, not only in the UK but abroad, that Brexit is inevitable. This is mainly because, for the first time, there is no effective parliamentary opposition to the party in power (although Mrs. May's Conservative parliamentary party is deeply divided by its 180 degree turn from supporting 'remain' under previous Prime Minister Cameron to mandatory support for 'leave' under her). And there is no even informal popular grouping for 'remain' which could demand attention.

So it is virtually impossible to place material showing that Article 50 can be avoided in the UK and foreign press. For example, when I complained to the New York Times both their correspondents in London made it clear that they had found nothing to cover, and the Chief Political Adviser to the BBC assured me that it would give proper coverage if there were any appreciable moves to avoid Brexit.

An effective opposition essential: an unmissable opportunity for a Labour & LibDem come back

There is though one obvious event which would instantly ensure full media coverage making the UK's predicament re Brexit known worldwide. That is for a disciplined Labour Party to resume its 'remain' policy during the referendum campaign. Jeremy Corbyn, its leader, has promised determined opposition to Mrs. May's Conservatives and it was he who made possibly the best speech for 'remain' during the election campaign on 14 May – notably calling for the UK to take the lead in reforming the EU wanted by so many countries (he urged members to be more concerned with social justice than remaining something of a capitalist club). All Corbyn needs to do now is to lead Labour's MPs in making a clear unified message opposing Brexit. Only opposition to Brexit can put Labour on the right side of history for Brexit will soon be seen as yesterday's folly. Then Labour would right away become a forceful opposition with a real possibility of returning to power.

Celebrities

And once there is forceful opposition to Brexit, UK and world media will make it known both in the UK and in the world. And once that happens, celebrities – far more influential than politicians - will lend their support. One of them, highly respected for her international concern, who had offered to back the case for 'avoid', withdrew because she did not want to find herself alone. Yet her agent told me there were several others on his books who would give their support if there were evident opposition to Mrs. May. For example just a sportsman, an Olympic gold medallist, an actor, and a best-selling author could do much to win over public opinion. If invited there would be several more.

'Remain' MPs now well placed to persuade others to join them

As many Labour supporters already recognise, the best hope for Labour to return to power is in coalition with the Liberal Democrats, not competing for seats. At the 8 December vote 23 Labour MPs and 5 LibDems including their leader, 'came out' against Brexit, along with the 51 members of the Scottish National Party, 3 from Wales' Plaid Cymru, and 3 from Northern Ireland's SDLP. Broad enough to encourage other MPs of all parties to 'come out' as the potential of Brexit for disaster becomes ever more apparent. Labour would recover its roots and the Libdems would recover the support they lost by their coalition with Cameron's Conservatives instead of Gordon Brown's Labour.

But if avoiding Brexit is to be generally accepted it is imperative that Labour does not allow Mrs. May to steal its clothes by trying to persuade 'leavers' that she has their interests at heart. Labour (and indeed any 'coalition' for 'avoid'), must convince 'leavers', who mostly are its natural supporters, that they will demand that the government address their grievances and will act with determination in government.

I must conclude with three points – the first is that Climate Change is by far the most important challenge that mankind faces and Trump does not recognise this. So one of the most important tasks for the UK within the EU is to work on this particularly with China which is well aware of this threat.

The second is to compare Mrs. May's approach to a Trump presidency with Mrs. Merkel's. In an attempt to preserve the so-called 'special relationship' with the US, Mrs. May is ready to bow to Trump even to the extent of arranging a state visit for him. This would be a nice feather to add to his cap – but no guarantee that he would prove a reliable friend to the UK. His approval of Brexit could be more closely related to his concern for his golf courses in Scotland – as the Scottish government has discovered! Far better is German Chancellor Mrs. Merkal's pointedly warning: 'yes' to cooperation, but only if Trump adheres to the norms expected of democratic states.

Thirdly – after my article of 2 November 2016 in Le Monde (about how Brexit could be avoided) feedback suggested that the Commission – and indeed all involved with Brexit, especially France and Germany with their elections this year, would be so relieved if Article 50 were not to be invoked that the UK would swiftly be able to negotiate the dispensations its very particular position in the EU demands – dispensations that would certainly be refused in Brexit negotiations. I suggest that some MPs should enquire if this can be confirmed.

Mr Rupert Murdoch: Iraq and the Ukraine

After our consideration of our first Brexiteer, UK Prime Minister Theresa May, and describing the Brexit phenomenon in my two reports we return to our consideration of our second Brexiteer Mr. Rupert Murdoch.

We mentioned above that he, as a leading supporter of the neo-conservatives through his ownership of their Weekly Standard and their Project for a New American Century (PNAC), had a hand in both the Iraq war and their interference in the Ukraine where Russia has a vital national interest - something the 'Anglosaxon' media almost entirely forgets.

To take the invasion of Iraq first – which as we saw led to the destabilisation of the Middle East, the re-opening of the Sunni/Shia schism, and the resultant civil war in Syria between the Alawite (neo-shia) government and Sunni insurgents, here are four papers which look at this neo-conservative attempt to bring unipolarism to the world – American global hegemony.

The first is my note: 'An inexcusable blunder that war on Iraq'.

The second is my letter published by The Independent on 10 September 2002, followed by my submission of 4 September which they did not accept. The third is New York Senator Hillary Clinton's (as she then was) speech of October2002 on the motion to invade Iraq. The fourth is Senator Byrd's speech against the invasion of 19 March 2003 just before it began.

After Murdoch's role in supporting the neo-Conservatives Unipolarist invasion of Iraq which destabilised the Middle East we shall need to consider his support for their Unipolarist meddling in the Ukraine which destabilised all of Europe – EU west and Russian east.

A BLUNDER, THAT VOTE FOR THE INVASION OF IRAQ WITHOUT UNITED NATIONS APPROVAL

My note of 3 August, 2008:

Destabilisation of the Middle East leading to the Syrian civil war, the EU refugee crisis which benefitted 'leave'.

We in the US and the UK got the Iraq war because of a failure of democracy. Both the Democrats in the United States' presidential system and the Conservatives in the UK's parliamentary system failed in their duty as opposition parties.

In the US House of Representatives on 10 October 2002 81 Democrats voted with Republicans to authorise the use of US armed forces against Iraq. The result: 296-133. In the Senate the next day the Yeas had it 77 – 23. Senator McCain the presumptive Republican candidate for the presidency, and Senators Edwards, Hillary Clinton, and Kerry all at one time Democratic candidates, voted yea. This despite a remarkable dissenting speech by Senator Byrd. It later emerged that not a few senators (notably including Mrs. Clinton) had not even read the secret papers on Iraq prepared for them in the senate library.

In the UK's House of Commons on 18 March 2003 the vote authorising 'the use of all means necessary to ensure Iraq's disarmament' passed 412 – 149. This despite an even more remarkable dissenting speech the previous day by Britain's former Foreign Secretary, Robin Cook. Some alledge that the new leader of the Conservative opposition, Iain Duncan Smith, had too readily believed Prime Minister Tony Blair in a private confidential briefing.

Only the Liberal Democrats voted as a party against the motion. Prime Minister Gordon Brown, then Chancellor of the Exchequer – one man whose opposition to the invasion might have prevented the UK's participation - voted for. So did Conservative Opposition leader David Cameron, then a back bencher (albeit 'reluctantly').

The sole candidate with a prospect of political leadership in the US or the UK to have opposed the Iraq war was Senator Barak Obama.

One searches the US and UK records in vain for a speech setting out the arguments against an invasion of Iraq without wide international support that we Cassandras were making. As is now becoming clear these were also being advanced by experts inside both the US and UK governments (e.g. see Ross Carne's testimony after he had resigned from the UK's Diplomatic Service).

Perhaps Brent Scowcroft, a key figure in Republican foreign policy, is the doyen of the Cassandras. An Air Force Lieutenant General he was Military Assistant to President Nixon, later National Security Adviser to both President Ford and President H.W. Bush. In his op-ed article in the Wall Street Journal for 15 August 2002 he remarks 'An attack on Iraq at this time would seriously jeopardize, if not destroy, the global counter-terrorist campaign we have undertaken.' He warned that war on Iraq would be a diversion from the 'war on terrorism'. This required wide international cooperation which risked being lost. Scowcroft advised there had first to be a resolution of the Israel/Palestine problem. An attack on Iraq could lead to destabilisation of the Arab regimes. Anti-terrorism (and so the campaign in Afghanistan) required continued top priority. 'A comprehensive perspective' on the international consequences of an invasion of Iraq was essential.

On the Democrat side Leon Fuerth, Al Gore's National Security Adviser during his Vice Presidency, with whom I exchanged views, added to Scowcroft's warnings the need to put North Korea before Iraq. His letter in the New York Times (4 January 2003) points out that 'the outcome of the administration's diplomacy is that America is preparing to fight a war with a country that might eventually acquire nuclear weapons, while another country is closing in on the ability to go into mass production'.

The senators, congressmen, and Members of Parliament all had greater access to the experts and the facts than did we outsiders. On this grave matter of war they all had the duty to probe thoroughly before casting their vote. Our unheeded warnings have, alas, all come true. (For my own claim to 'Cassandraship' see e.g. my letter to the Independent of 10 September 2002 beginning: 'Isn't a US attack on Iraq just what Osama bin Laden's flagging plan requires?)

We Cassandras pointed out that 9/11 was not a 'Pearl Habour' – an attack to destroy a vital element of the adversary's military power at the opening of hostilities – rather a ju jitsu ploy to provoke a wildly disproportionate response, so using the adversary's own strength to bring about a fall. So President G.W. Bush's carefully prepared and professionally executed invasion of Afghanistan with widespread international support (or at least tacit acceptance) had denied Al Qaeda the rash reaction it had expected.

Clearly what was required was continued top priority for cadres, finance, and forces to ensure Afghanistan's stabilisation and reconstruction after decades of destruction (no easy task given that country's history). This needed to be paralleled with a determined attempt to resolve the Palestine/Israel problem which provided Al Qaeda with so much of the Arab resentment on which it depended for support and recruits. For this, as 2002 ended, there had never been such widespread international support.

With the astonishing support that Robin Cook noted, the world was near to establishing the era of international cooperation that the end of the Cold War had made possible. World cooperation on international terrorism and wide support for ending the Israel/Palestine running sore on the international scene, could be harbingers for cooperation on other problems requiring international cooperation from North Korea to climate change.

But Vice President Cheney, and the neo-conservatives placed in key positions in the G.W. Bush administration, saw things differently. They were concerned to ensure US dominance in the 21st century – their 'think tank' was called The Project for a New American Century.

For them an invasion of Iraq would not be a diversion from the 'War on Terror' but a means of winning it. For it would:

1. overthrow a hated dictator, so winning kudos in the Middle East and among Human Rights activists.

2. eliminate such WMD as Iraq possessed – a warning to North Korea and others like Iran that might be tempted to acquire the bomb.

3. secure Iraq's oil – especially important given doubts about the stability of Saudi Arabia, home of Bin Laden's extremist Wahabism.

4. obtain permanent US bases in Iraq – unacceptable in Saudi Arabia. So achieving US military dominance at the heart of the Middle East.

5. establish an American style democracy in Iraq, the success of which would be imitated, creating a New Middle East.

6. replace a hostile with a friendly Iraq, much improving Israel's security and its bargaining position with the Palestinians, Syria and others.

7. demonstrate by 'shock and awe' to all the world US overwhelming military and economic might – its ability to go anywhere, pay any

price, to ensure that the 21st would indeed be an American Century – the key aim of the neo-conservatives

And added after 9/11:

8. To trump Al Qaeda in its Islamic heartland - effectively winning the 'war on terror' by ending its prestige and dashing its hopes of re-making the Middle East in its own extremist Wahabist image.

This beguiling scenario – though the administration stressed only 1. and 2. – could be deduced from neo-conservative writings and the remarks of those 'embedded' in the Pentagon and other parts of the administration. Only a handful of politicians challenged its assumptions though many experts in and out of government did.

First, they pointed out, hopes of this sort for the Iraq operation ignored the reality on the ground. Iraq is fissiparous – ethnic Kurds, Arabs etc.; religious Shi'ites, Sunnis, and others (including Christians). The history of British rule after creating this artificial country following World War I suggested that only a firm leader could hold it together. So a strong occupation force and a firm interim administration would be essential to prevent chaotic collapse.

General Eric Shinseki, Chief of Staff of the US Army during the run up to war, famously told the Senate Armed Forces Committee that "something of the order of several hundred thousand soldiers" would probably be needed for this purpose. After Defense Secretary Rumsfeld and his deputy Paul Wolfowitz (a leading neo-conservative) pooh poohed this, Shinseki's testimony was ignored. Yet already in the summer of 2002 the British government had itself expressed much concern at the lack of planning for an occupation.

Second, both Bush and Blair had to present a cheap quick war in order to get the political approvals they needed. That meant adopting the

Rumsfeld lite force, and claiming that the whole operation would cost only $50-100bn. The Shinseki alternative involved a far bigger, far more expensive operation – probably impossible given the commitment in Afghanistan.

==

Opposing Brexit. The Independent (London), 10 September, 2002 (My letter)

'Sir: Isn't a US attack on Iraq just what Osama bin Laden's flagging plan requires? After 11 September it was widely suspected that al-Qa'ida's plan was to provoke a massive ill-directed, unilateral, anti-Muslim retaliation from the United States. This would release extremist Islamic forces, destabilising the already precarious Middle East and compromising the West's oil supply. That in turn would create economic and political havoc in the developed world. When the dust eventually settled a new extremist Islam would face a debilitated West.

'With political skill and military luck the Bush administration avoided such a scenario with a measured, internationally accepted response in Afghanistan. Now though, the President is squandering the world's good will in a series of unilateral actions. He declines to ensure stability in Afghanistan, and refuses his vital support in settling the Israel/Palestine problem on the lines now acceptable to all interested nations.

'In these circumstances a war in Iraq, followed by some questionable nation-building, makes 11 September look like a gamble al-Qa'ida might yet win.   John Pedler
Volosko, Croatia'

Here is my 4 September 2002 analysis prepared in consultation with one of Al Gore's former National Security Advisers. It also was submitted to The Independent but was not accepted:-

Ten reasons why Iraq must not be invaded without UN approval (my submission to The Independent, 4 September 2002)

Collecting the views of experts in the various fields who are not involved in supporting the present U.S. administration or the U.K. government, we find the following principal objections to an invasion of Iraq without Security Council approval (which is unlikely to be obtainable):-

i) **Afghanistan**: it could well undermine success in Afghanistan. It would be folly to start a second, elective, war before Afghanistan has been secured, a new government has won general support, warlords are tamed, and reconstruction is safely underway. Afghanistan would lose its top priority to Iraq both for manpower, finance, and other resources - e.g. expertise on Islam and terrorism. Without prompt definitive success in stabilising Afghanistan, al Qaeda and the Taliban could once again return to use it.

ii) **Worldwide backing**: it risks losing the quite remarkable worldwide support, both political and financial, which President G W Bush has enjoyed for the occupation of Afghanistan since Al Qaeda's "9/11" attacks on the US. This support is essential to uprooting al Qaeda style international terrorism.

iii) **Culture clash**: the invasion of a second Muslim country must surely further Al Qaeda's major aim with its "9/11" attacks of provoking the profound clash of cultures it needs if it is to win wide Muslim support. Such a clash must be avoided if Al Qaeda is to be isolated within the Muslim world.

iv) **Al Qaeda's home turf**: Saddam Hussein has kept Al Qaeda out of Iraq. With Saddam gone it would surely strive to get in and cause mayhem. Once in Iraq Al Qaeda would be back on its Arabic Middle Eastern home ground only one frontier away from Saudi Arabia, its prime target for destabilisation.

v) **Splitting allies**: without UN approval, an invasion would all but certainly split NATO, Europe and the largely united Western presence in the UN. This would not only affect the outcome of the occupation in Afghanistan, but the standing and influence of the West in the Middle East and indeed, throughout the world.

vi) **No nuclear threat**: it would be folly to invade Iraq (which virtually all experts agree has no nuclear weapons) in order to prevent nuclear proliferation, instead of focussing, with the riparian states, on reversing the nuclear programme of North Korea which is well on the way to possessing a nuclear bomb.

vii) **Iraq is fissiparous**: If Saddam Hussein is removed Sunnis (now dominant), majority Shi'as (repressed), Kurds (who would prefer independence) and other disgruntled groups, would all seek to protect and forward their interests risking grave civil disturbance, even internecine strife - should any invasion not be accompanied by a carefully prepared transfer of power and swift departure. But it appears that the UK (whose participation the U.S. seeks) is still far from satisfied that post-invasion policy has been meticulously and wisely planned.

viii) **American hegemony**: such an invasion would be seen by many (notably Russia and China) as an American attempt to dominate the Middle East and thus secure US world hegemony in the 21st century. (The "neo-conservative movement" calls itself The Project for A New American Century. Vice-President Cheney and several other "neo-conservatives" are in key positions in the G W Bush administration).

Such a U.S. move for world dominance would be counter-productive. It is not the way for the US - the remaining superpower - to lead the world towards the international cooperation so essential in the post-Cold War era.

ix) **Iran, the Arabs & Israel**: putting American forces to the west as well as to the east of Iran must lead to conflict with Iran for influence in Iraq and strain - or end - the nascent cooperation between the US & Iran with the overthrow of the Taliban, the common enemy. Saddam's Sunni secular Iraq (backed by the West) waged war on Iran for 8 years with tremendous World War I style losses. Iran will be out to exercise all possible influence over any new regime in Iraq, and Shias in the Sunni states. This would cause tension between Shia revolutionary Iran and Iraq's Sunni neighbours as well as with the U.S. There is a grave risk of destabilising the entire Middle East- which would seriously undermine Israel's security - and of course the safety of the Christian minorities in the Middle East.

x) **Climate change, etc**: The international disruption to be expected from such an invasion of Iraq would distract world attention from the existential threats that humanity now faces: Climate Destabilisation a Human Rights and much else - all of which require world cooperation.

Conclusion: These ten objections alone make an "unapproved" invasion far too high risk to be acceptable. This could change if a) continued world support - military and financial - demonstrates that the reconstruction and stabilisation of Afghanistan is on the way to irreversible success, and if b) the main recruiting source for al Qaeda - worldwide Muslim bitterness at Palestinian woes - is removed by an Israel/Palestine agreement which should now be the top priority for the Middle East. "9/11" plus the successful occupation of Afghanistan with such worldwide backing makes an Israeli/Palestine settlement far more possible than it has ever been before.

All these ten reasons for not now invading Iraq are clearly valid and there for all to see. It is deeply disturbing that our leaders so far appear either blind to them, or are determined on an Iraq invasion regardless of the unacceptable risk.

THE PRO & THECONTRA OF INVADING IRAQ. PRO: SENATOR HILLARY CLINTON'S SPEECH, CONTRA: SENATOR BYRD'S SPEECH

SENATOR CLINTON, 10 OCTOBER 2002

Today we are asked whether to give the President of the United States authority to use force in Iraq should diplomatic efforts fail to dismantle Saddam Hussein's chemical and biological weapons and his nuclear program.

I am honored to represent nearly 19 million New Yorkers, a thoughtful democracy of voices and opinions who make themselves heard on the great issues of our day especially this one. Many have contacted my office about this resolution, both in support of and in opposition to it, and I am grateful to all who have expressed an opinion.

I also greatly respect the differing opinions within this body. The debate they engender will aid our search for a wise, effective policy. Therefore, on no account should dissent be discouraged or disparaged. It is central to our freedom and to our progress, for on more than one occasion, history has proven our great dissenters to be right.

Now, I believe the facts that have brought us to this fateful vote are not in doubt. Saddam Hussein is a tyrant who has tortured and killed his own people, even his own family members, to maintain his iron grip on power. He used chemical weapons on Iraqi Kurds and on Iranians, killing over 20 thousand people. Unfortunately, during the

1980's, while he engaged in such horrific activity, he enjoyed the support of the American government, because he had oil and was seen as a counterweight to the Ayatollah Khomeini in Iran.

In 1991, Saddam Hussein invaded and occupied Kuwait, losing the support of the United States. The first President Bush assembled a global coalition, including many Arab states, and threw Saddam out after forty-three days of bombing and a hundred hours of ground operations. The U.S.-led coalition then withdrew, leaving the Kurds and the Shiites, who had risen against Saddam Hussein at our urging, to Saddam's revenge.

As a condition for ending the conflict, the United Nations imposed a number of requirements on Iraq, among them disarmament of all weapons of mass destruction, stocks used to make such weapons, and laboratories necessary to do the work. Saddam Hussein agreed, and an inspection system was set up to ensure compliance. And though he repeatedly lied, delayed, and obstructed the inspections work, the inspectors found and destroyed far more weapons of mass destruction capability than were destroyed in the Gulf War, including thousands of chemical weapons, large volumes of chemical and biological stocks, a number of missiles and warheads, a major lab equipped to produce anthrax and other bio-weapons, as well as substantial nuclear facilities.

In 1998, Saddam Hussein pressured the United Nations to lift the sanctions by threatening to stop all cooperation with the inspectors. In an attempt to resolve the situation, the UN, unwisely in my view, agreed to put limits on inspections of designated "sovereign sites" including the so-called presidential palaces, which in reality were huge compounds well suited to hold weapons labs, stocks, and records which Saddam Hussein was required by UN resolution to turn over. When Saddam blocked the inspection process, the inspectors left. As a result, President Clinton, with the British and others, ordered an intensive four-day air assault, Operation Desert

Fox, on known and suspected weapons of mass destruction sites and other military targets.

In 1998, the United States also changed its underlying policy toward Iraq from containment to regime change and began to examine options to effect such a change, including support for Iraqi opposition leaders within the country and abroad.

In the four years since the inspectors left, intelligence reports show that Saddam Hussein has worked to rebuild his chemical and biological weapons stock, his missile delivery capability, and his nuclear program. He has also given aid, comfort, and sanctuary to terrorists, including Al Qaeda members, though there is apparently no evidence of his involvement in the terrible events of September 11, 2001.

It is clear, however, that if left unchecked, Saddam Hussein will continue to increase his capacity to wage biological and chemical warfare, and will keep trying to develop nuclear weapons. Should he succeed in that endeavor, he could alter the political and security landscape of the Middle East, which as we know all too well affects American security.

Now this much is undisputed. The open questions are: what should we do about it? How, when, and with whom?

Some people favor attacking Saddam Hussein now, with any allies we can muster, in the belief that one more round of weapons inspections would not produce the required disarmament, and that deposing Saddam would be a positive good for the Iraqi people and would create the possibility of a secular democratic state in the Middle East, one which could perhaps move the entire region toward democratic reform.

This view has appeal to some, because it would assure disarmament; because it would right old wrongs after our abandonment of the Shiites and Kurds in 1991, and our support for Saddam Hussein in the 1980's when he was using chemical weapons and terrorizing his people; and because it would give the Iraqi people a chance to build a future in freedom.

However, this course is fraught with danger. We and our NATO allies did not depose Mr. Milosevic, who was responsible for more than a quarter of a million people being killed in the 1990s. Instead, by stopping his aggression in Bosnia and Kosovo, and keeping on the tough sanctions, we created the conditions in which his own people threw him out and led to his being in the dock being tried for war crimes as we speak.

If we were to attack Iraq now, alone or with few allies, it would set a precedent that could come back to haunt us. In recent days, Russia has talked of an invasion of Georgia to attack Chechen rebels. India has mentioned the possibility of a pre-emptive strike on Pakistan. And what if China were to perceive a threat from Taiwan?

So Mr. President, for all its appeal, a unilateral attack, while it cannot be ruled out, on the present facts is not a good option.

Others argue that we should work through the United Nations and should only resort to force if and when the United Nations Security Council approves it. This too has great appeal for different reasons. The UN deserves our support. Whenever possible we should work through it and strengthen it, for it enables the world to share the risks and burdens of global security and when it acts, it confers a legitimacy that increases the likelihood of long-term success. The UN can help lead the world into a new era of global cooperation and the United States should support that goal.

But there are problems with this approach as well. The United Nations is an organization that is still growing and maturing. It often lacks the cohesion to enforce its own mandates. And when Security Council members use the veto, on occasion, for reasons of narrow-minded interests, it cannot act. In Kosovo, the Russians did not approve NATO military action because of political, ethnic, and religious ties to the Serbs. The United States therefore could not obtain a Security Council resolution in favor of the action necessary to stop the dislocation and ethnic cleansing of more than a million Kosovar Albanians. However, most of the world was with us because there was a genuine emergency with thousands dead and a million driven from their homes. As soon as the American-led conflict was over, Russia joined the peacekeeping effort that is still underway.

In the case of Iraq, recent comments indicate that one or two Security Council members might never approve force against Saddam Hussein until he has actually used chemical, biological, or God forbid, nuclear weapons.

So, Mr. President, the question is how do we do our best to both defuse the real threat that Saddam Hussein poses to his people, to the region, including Israel, to the United States, to the world, and at the same time, work to maximize our international support and strengthen the United Nations?

While there is no perfect approach to this thorny dilemma, and while people of good faith and high intelligence can reach diametrically opposed conclusions, I believe the best course is to go to the UN for a strong resolution that scraps the 1998 restrictions on inspections and calls for complete, unlimited inspections with cooperation expected and demanded from Iraq. I know that the Administration wants more, including an explicit authorization to use force, but we may not be able to secure that now, perhaps even later. But if we get a clear requirement for unfettered inspections, I believe the authority to use force to enforce that mandate is inherent in the original 1991 UN resolution, as President Clinton recognized when he launched Operation Desert Fox in 1998.

If we get the resolution that President Bush seeks, and if Saddam complies, disarmament can proceed and the threat can be eliminated. Regime change will, of course, take longer but we must still work for it, nurturing all reasonable forces of opposition.

If we get the resolution and Saddam does not comply, then we can attack him with far more support and legitimacy than we would have otherwise.

If we try and fail to get a resolution that simply, but forcefully, calls for Saddam's compliance with unlimited inspections, those who oppose even that will be in an indefensible position. And, we will still have more support and legitimacy than if we insist now on a resolution that includes authorizing military action and other requirements giving some nations superficially legitimate reasons to oppose any Security Council action. They will say we never wanted a resolution at all and that we only support the United Nations when it does exactly what we want.

I believe international support and legitimacy are crucial. After shots are fired and bombs are dropped, not all consequences are predictable. While the military outcome is not in doubt, should we put troops on the ground, there is still the matter of Saddam Hussein's biological and chemical weapons. Today he has maximum incentive not to use them or give them away. If he did either, the world would demand his immediate removal. Once the battle is joined, however, with the outcome certain, he will have maximum incentive to use weapons of mass destruction and to give what he can't use to terrorists who can torment us with them long after he is gone. We cannot be paralyzed by this possibility, but we would be foolish to ignore it. And according to recent reports, the CIA agrees with this analysis. A world united in sharing the risk at least would make this occurrence less likely and more bearable and would be far more likely to share with us the considerable burden of rebuilding a secure and peaceful post-Saddam Iraq.

President Bush's speech in Cincinnati and the changes in policy that have come forth since the Administration began broaching this issue some weeks ago have made my vote easier. Even though the resolution before the Senate is not as strong as I would like in requiring the diplomatic route first and placing highest priority on a simple, clear requirement for unlimited inspections, I will take the President at his word that he will try hard to pass a UN resolution and will seek to avoid war, if at all possible.

Because bipartisan support for this resolution makes success in the United Nations more likely, and therefore, war less likely, and because a good faith effort by the United States, even if it fails, will bring more allies and legitimacy to our cause, I have concluded, after careful and serious consideration, that a vote for the resolution best serves the security of our nation. If we were to defeat this resolution or pass it with only a few Democrats, I am concerned that those who want to pretend this problem will go way with delay will oppose any UN resolution calling for unrestricted inspections.

This is a very difficult vote. This is probably the hardest decision I have ever had to make -- any vote that may lead to war should be hard -- but I cast it with conviction.

And perhaps my decision is influenced by my eight years of experience on the other end of Pennsylvania Avenue in the White House watching my husband deal with serious challenges to our nation. I want this President, or any future President, to be in the strongest possible position to lead our country in the United Nations or in war. Secondly, I want to insure that Saddam Hussein makes no mistake about our national unity and for our support for the President's efforts to wage America's war against terrorists and weapons of mass destruction. And thirdly, I want the men and women in our Armed Forces to know that if they should be called upon to act against Iraq, our country will stand resolutely behind them.

My vote is not, however, a vote for any new doctrine of pre-emption, or for uni-lateralism, or for the arrogance of American power or purpose - all of which carry grave dangers for our nation, for the rule of international law and for the peace and security of people throughout the world.

Over eleven years have passed since the UN called on Saddam Hussein to rid himself of weapons of mass destruction as a condition of returning to the world community. Time and time again he has frustrated and denied these conditions. This matter cannot be left hanging forever with consequences we would all live to regret. War can yet be avoided, but our responsibility to global security and to the integrity of United Nations resolutions protecting it cannot. I urge the President to spare no effort to secure a clear, unambiguous demand by the United Nations for unlimited inspections.

And finally, on another personal note, I come to this decision from the perspective of a Senator from New York who has seen all too closely the consequences of last year's terrible attacks on our nation. In balancing the risks of action versus inaction, I think New Yorkers who have gone through the fires of hell may be more attuned to the risk of not acting. I know that I am.

So it is with conviction that I support this resolution as being in the best interests of our nation. A vote for it is not a vote to rush to war; it is a vote that puts awesome responsibility in the hands of our President and we say to him - use these powers wisely and as a last resort. And it is a vote that says clearly to Saddam Hussein - this is your last chance - disarm or be disarmed.

Thank you, Mr. President.

==

Pro and contra re invading Iraq: pro Senator Robert Byrd

"Today, I weep for my country"

On the afternoon of March 19, 2003, mere hours before bombs began falling in Baghdad, Sen. Robert Byrd, D-W.Va., gave a speech on the floor of the U.S. Senate condemning the use of military force in Iraq.

Senator Byrd I believe in this beautiful country. I have studied its roots and gloried in the wisdom of its magnificent Constitution. I have marveled at the wisdom of its founders and framers. Generation after generation of Americans has understood the lofty ideals that underlie our great Republic. I have been inspired by the story of their sacrifice and their strength.

But, today I weep for my country. I have watched the events of recent months with a heavy, heavy heart. No more is the image of America one of strong, yet benevolent peacekeeper. The image of America has changed. Around the globe, our friends mistrust us, our word is disputed, our intentions are questioned.

Instead of reasoning with those with whom we disagree, we demand obedience or threaten recrimination. Instead of isolating Saddam Hussein we seem to have isolated ourselves. We proclaim a new doctrine of preemption which is understood by few and feared by many. We say that the United States has the right to turn its firepower on any corner of the globe which might be suspect in the war on terrorism. We assert that right without the sanction of any international body. As a result, the world has become a much more dangerous place.

We flaunt our superpower status with arrogance. We treat U.N. Security Council members like ingrates who offend our princely dignity by lifting their heads from the carpet. Valuable alliances are split. After war has ended, the United States will have to rebuild much more than the country of Iraq. We will have to rebuild America's image around the globe.

The case this Administration tries to make to justify its fixation with war is tainted by charges of falsified documents and circumstantial evidence. We cannot convince the world of the necessity of this war for one simple reason. This is a war of choice.

There is no credible information to connect Saddam Hussein to 9/11. The twin towers fell because a world-wide terrorist group, al-Qaida, with cells in over 60 nations, struck at our wealth and our influence by turning our own planes into missiles, one of which would likely have slammed into the dome of this beautiful Capitol except for the brave sacrifice of the passengers on board.

The brutality seen on September 11th and in other terrorist attacks we have witnessed around the globe are the violent and desperate efforts by extremists to stop the daily encroachment of western values upon their cultures. That is what we fight. It is a force not confined to borders. It is a shadowy entity with many faces, many names, and many addresses.

But, this Administration has directed all of the anger, fear, and grief which emerged from the ashes of the twin towers and the twisted metal of the Pentagon towards a tangible villain, one we can see and hate and attack. And villain he is. But, he is the wrong villain. And this is the wrong war. If we attack Saddam Hussein, we will probably drive him from power. But, the zeal of our friends to assist our global war on terrorism may have already taken flight.

The general unease surrounding this war is not just due to "orange alert." There is a pervasive sense of rush and risk and too many questions unanswered. How long will we be in Iraq? What will be the cost? What is the ultimate mission? How great is the danger at home? A pall has fallen over the Senate Chamber. We avoid our solemn duty to debate the one topic on the minds of all Americans, even while scores of thousands of our sons and daughters faithfully do their duty in Iraq.

What is happening to this country? When did we become a nation which ignores and berates our friends? When did we decide to risk undermining international order by adopting a radical and doctrinaire approach to using our awesome military might? How can we abandon diplomatic efforts when the turmoil in the world cries out for diplomacy?

Why can this President not seem to see that America's true power lies not in its will to intimidate, but in its ability to inspire?

War appears inevitable. But, I continue to hope that the cloud will lift. Perhaps Saddam will yet turn tail and run. Perhaps reason will somehow still prevail. I along with millions of Americans will pray for the safety of our troops, for the innocent civilians in Iraq, and for the security of our homeland. May God continue to bless the United States of America in the troubled days ahead, and may we somehow recapture the vision which for the present eludes us.

===

Mr. Murdoch and the Neo-Conservatives – Iraq and the Ukraine I return to Rupert Murdoch and President G. W. Bush's Vice President Cheney leader of the neo-conservatives. Following the election of Barak Obama in 2008 they went to ground while at the same time planning their next move. They came back surreptitiously under Hilary Clinton, Obama's Secretary of State, more to heal the division among Democrats, many of whom had supported Clinton's bid for the Presidency, than because he approved of her interventionist foreign policy – as over the Iraq war. He did not, but clearly hoped to be able to keep her in check. He did not.

He was of course engrossed with resolving the daunting problems he inherited from his predecessor G.W. Bush: the worst financial crisis since the Great Depression in the 1930s and the two wars in Iraq and Afghanistan which as we have seen destabilised the Middle East with such serious consequences – even influencing the June 2016 UK referendum. And at the pinnacle of power a politician depends on his 'gatekeepers' all along the line right up to his Chief of Staff – then Rahm Emmanuel. But anywhere information for the President goes up the ladder a neo-conservative sympathiser could have blocked the news of their revival. Clearly Hilary Clinton did not warn Obama but someone who should have reported this surreptitious resurrection evidently did not.

Mr. Murdoch's support for the Neo-Conservative Unipolar intervention in Russia continues to undermine attempts to present the Russian reality and its immense importance for the EU – and the UK. In an attempt to correct the current misinformation about this and the Putin/Trump relationship I have selected some important articles sandwiched between my own comments.

==

PRESIDENT PUTIN AND PRESIDENT TRUMP

As I have said, I am considering both together because it is 'their world' that is the background to our times. Both present threats to the EU and the UK which make it all the more essential that the UK remains in the EU to resolve the many complex problems that they bring. With the advent of President Trump America's place in the world was profoundly altered requiring the UK and the EU to adapt together to this rupture with the status quo since World War II when the US was the unchallenged leader of the 'free world' despite grievous mistakes.

Putin and Trump are inextricably linked by the former's intervention in the 2016 US Presidential election. This did not come out the blue but goes back to Western policies towards Russia after the collapse of the Soviet Union. So it is important to look back at this history. First here's a paper of mine this is followed by at some of the most relevant articles of others.

==

NATO, the West and Putin's Russia

We publish again today (12 June 2012) our piece on NATO, Putin, and the possibility of improved relations with Russia - it remains just as timely in this first year of Putin's second presidency.

Russia and Europe: friend or foe?

As the Georgia crisis continues amid wide denunciation of Russia, it is important to remember the fundamentals of Russia's relations with the countries of the European Union.

Russia is culturally, historically, and in its most important area a European country and Russians consider themselves a European people. At least since Peter the Great in the 17th Century moulded his country on European lines, Russia has played a major role in Europe's history, notably in the defeat of both Napoleon and Nazi Germany.

One cannot imagine today's European culture without Russian classical music and ballet, and its literature and poetry – to mention only composers Prokoviev, Tchaikov News, Rachmaninov and Shostakovich, and writers Pushkin, Tolstoy, Dostoevsky, Pasternak, and Solzhenitsin. Christianity too, is basic to Russian culture – for hundreds of years Russians defended the Christian faith against numerous forces – notably the Golden Hoarde. The Russian Orthodox and Catholic churches share essentially the same theology despite a millennium of priestly disputes.

Russia temporarily left the European fold with the Bolshevik Revolution, Stalin's purges, and the Cold War. Since the fall of the Soviet Union the Russian people – even the only moderately affluent - have to a large extent reintegrated with Europeans with whom they feel more at home than with any other people.

Unfortunately – because the European Union has no united voice in world affairs - it was not fellow European countries but the United States that played the dominant role in Western policy towards Russia after the fall of the Soviet Union. So American laissez faire capitalism, not the EU's more controlled capitalism with its emphasis on welfare, was adopted in the chaotic and socially divided Russia of President Yeltsin.

The result was the return to authoritarianism under Vladimir Putin – welcomed by the bulk of Russians who were suffering worse economic conditions than under Gorbachev's USSR. The so-abrupt descent from super-power status was far more humiliating for Russians than, say, for the British whose descent from world dominance took place over half a century. But when Gorbachev declared the end of the Cold War, the Russian Federation that emerged remained a great power – "the only power capable of destroying the United States".

With the collapse of the Soviet Union President G.H.W. Bush carried on President Reagan's policy of détente with the Start I treaty (Strategic Arms Control), ratified in 1992, and the signature of the Start II treaty (Strategic Arms Reduction). At first NATO had no plans to expand eastwards after the fall of the Berlin wall, but agreement had to be reached once the DDR in East Germany came to an end, to ensure that all of a unified Germany remained militarily tied to the West. So, with Russian consent, NATO came to include eastern Germany. It was to end there.

According to Gorbachev (he repeated this recently) after the fall of the Berlin Wall the US (under G.H.W. Bush) pledged not to expand NATO to include the East European countries. That there was any binding pledge is though denied by Robert B. Zoellick who was at the time a State Department officer concerned with negotiations with the USSR. Whatever the nature of the understanding, there was soon a major debate in the US and in NATO countries about the wisdom of expanding NATO to the former Warsaw Pact countries and hence to the old Soviet frontier against Russian opposition. The question was: why raise Russian suspicions and risk the partnership it offered the

West, when NATO had only come into being to counter the threat from a Soviet Union that no longer existed?

But the US and some others saw NATO as the essential structure binding Europe and the US and Canada politically as well as militarily – a solution acceptable to Russia. But soon the drive for NATO's expansion eastwards began under President Clinton – at the 1997 Madrid Summit, the membership of Poland, Czechoslovakia and Hungary was accepted over the opposition of a still weak Russia. Still, Russia continued cooperation with the West on several issues while warning against further expansion which it would see as a threat.

America's move away from a new era of cooperation made possible by the end of the Cold War, towards a unipolar world dominated by the US, alarmed not only Russia but China. One major turning point from (diminished) cooperation to (open) confrontation came on 15 June 2001, when President G.W. Bush announced the intention to expand NATO to all the former Warsaw Pact countries. That same day Russia, China and some central Asian countries established the Shanghai Cooperation Organisation (SCO) as the 'new security concept' – i.e. to counter US unipolarism.

Then, less than 3 months later came '9/11' and there was a brief return towards co-operation: Russia and China also had problems with Muslim minorities and an interest in countering international terrorism.

But this evaporated with Bush's famous Axis of Evil Speech in January 2002 after which it soon became clear that the US would invade Iraq primarily to achieve a dominating military and political position in the Middle East – a point insufficiently understood in the West. This has been thwarted. Instead the occupation of Iraq has had the effect not only of increasing Iran's influence in Iraq and also the Middle East despite Sunni/Shia differences, but in greatly reducing Russia's (and

China's) fears of a New American Century (the name of the neo-conservative think tank). Over-extended militarily, financially strapped, and losing thanks to the Iraq war its hope of establishing a unipolar world, the US is now seen by Russia as becoming, not a paper tiger for its power and influence remain immense, but simply as another great power which can successfully be confronted. As for NATO, Russia sees the fissures in that organisation widening as its first 'out of area' operation in Afghanistan threatens to end in defeat.

Despite a fairly promising start under President G.H.W. Bush, President Clinton failed properly to follow up the partnership option with Russia. Russia was largely ignored, and its real national interest regarding its 'near abroad' was disregarded in favour of an unnecessary and provocative expansion of NATO.

By the autumn of 2007 it was already clear that not only was the US overstretched militarily, but that it was in deep and deepening financial trouble. On 2 October 2007, against this background of American decline, President Putin made a key speech on Russian foreign policy at the 43rd Munich Conference on Security Policy. (It was largely written off in the West as anti-American ranting but it deserves to be read by anyone concerned with European/Russian relations). He rejected both the concept and the possibility of an American unipolar world. He referred to the failure of America's "almost uncontained hyper use of force.... plunging the world into an abyss of permanent conflicts... Finding a political solution settlement also becomes almost impossible". He strongly criticised NATO's pretentions. At the end of his carefully prepared and reasonable speech he said – "And of course we would like to interact with responsible and independent partners with whom we can work together in constructing a fair and democratic world order that would ensure security and prosperity not only for a select few, but for all".

Whatever one's views of Mr. Putin and Russia, this speech surely deserved to be followed up to establish how sincere the Russian Federation was about this offer of collaboration in place of confrontation.

But sadly, the Europeans – still divided by the Iraq war and associated unipolarism – made no coordinated move to do this. As for the United States, the response came from President G.W. Bush on 3 April 2008 when he pressed NATO to accept as members Ukraine, Georgia and Afghanistan – this against the opposition of France and Germany.

To sum up, we in the West baited an apparently friendly bear and got a slap from its paw – largely as a result of NATO expansion coupled with our failure to ensure that the Georgian government acted with the utmost restraint while Europe and America mounted a joint effort to defuse the long standing tension over Abkhasia and over South Ossetia (an area divided by Stalin from its northern half).

Is it too late to test the sincerity of Russia's offer of joining in the cooperative era made possible by the fall of the Soviet Union? I believe not, for Russia's long term national interest and orientation is towards the closest possible relations with Europe. But there are two pre-conditions – the next US President, whatever he has to say as a candidate to satisfy 'patriotism', must make it clear that – facing up to America's decline during the disastrous G.W. Bush years – that the unipolar, hegemonistic, neo-conservative period is over and that the US now seeks to lead in creating a cooperative era.

Second, the European Union must find a single voice for the most important aspects of its international relations. This too, is not impossible even though the Union is currently all but paralysed over what sort of Union it should eventually be. On the great issue of world cooperation or confrontation all members of the Union have basically the same interest. The problem lies with members understandably afraid of Russia, and members who believe American unipolarism has been proved to be a step too far. If Russia is sincere about cooperation should America clearly renounce unipolarism, then the split among the Europeans would be healed. The way towards a partnership with Russia would be opened.

==

'Why is MI5 Making Such a Fuss over Russia

2 November 2016. Mary Dejevsky, The Guardian

Lenin once said: "The capitalists will sell us the rope with which we will hang them." Vladimir Putin is no Lenin, nor can his regime – run by an elite that enjoys offshore accounts and oligarchic privileges – quite be described as anti-capitalist. Yet in Russia's new confrontation with the west, the Kremlin's strategy is to exploit western weaknesses and confusion as much as it is geared towards showing a bellicose face, whether in Ukraine, Syria or cyberspace. Perhaps this is why the head of MI5 has warned of the need to fend off Russia's hostile interference. Lenin is not Putin's ideological guru. Foreigners, whether public officials or investors, who have at length met with Putin sometimes point to his particular brand of pragmatism (even if Angela Merkel once said he "lives in another world"). If he senses strong pushback, he adapts. If he detects gaps, he strikes at the Achilles heel.

There is little doubt Russian power is on the offensive. Since 2014, when it deployed its troops in Ukraine and annexed territory there, and since its policies in Syria have been analysed as overtly hostile to western endeavours, "Russian aggressiveness" has become a mainstay of the west's official political discourse. But beyond boasting about Russia's nuclear forces, demonstrating its new conventional military capacities and activating an army of internet trollers (none of which should be minimised), Putin's regime is banking on the hope that western democracies will falter and be unable to offer up genuine resistance - because in Russian eyes it has the potential to divide the west. The growth of national-populist movements in Europe and elsewhere is another, because it echoes the Kremlin's illiberal narrative and produces useful allies. Radical leftwing anti-Americanism also fits handily into the picture, as it did decades ago when pacifists demonstrated in the west while missiles were being deployed by the eastern bloc during the cold war.

As paradoxical as it is, the far right and the far left in Europe today join forces when it comes to Russia. The far right sees virtues in Putin; they are fascinated by his strong-man image, the ultra-conservative Christian values he espouses, and by a hostility they share towards Muslims. The far left sees a leader unfairly demonised, an underdog able to counter the greater evil of "western neo-imperialism" – whatever Russia's behaviour in its own former empire. The failure of politicians such as Jeremy Corbyn and Jean-Luc Melanchon (the Labour leader's closest equivalent on the French left) to clearly denounce Russia's massacring of civilians in Aleppo points to the kind of complacency, or silence, that Moscow is keen to capitalise on.

For a decade and a half, the west had its eyes set solely on the threat of international terrorism. Now it finds itself having to focus on a state threat also. Identifying the exact nature and extent of the Russian threat, and what should be done about it, are issues still being debated in Europe and during the US election. But to claim that Nato and western security agencies are deliberately exaggerating the danger coming from Russia for self-serving purposes (such as pumping up their budgets) is simply side-stepping a problem that cannot be denied.

If anyone needs to be convinced of this, travelling to the Baltic region might offer valuable insights. At a recent international conference I attended in Latvia's capital, Riga, much of the talk centred understandably on the strengthening of western defence guarantees (Nato countries are set to deploy four battalions in Poland and the three Baltic states by June 2017). It might be tempting to cast this move as open "provocation" towards Russia, but it is less so if you visit

Riga's Museum of Occupations, where one small nation's history of being invaded and persecuted by large powers (Nazi Germany and the Soviet Union) is vividly recounted.

Yet what I found most striking was Latvian officials saying that in Russia's reported attempts to interfere with this US election there were echoes of the Kremlin meddling in their own elections over the years. "We might have useful experiences to share on that account," is the comment. Baltic governments are making strong efforts to counter Russian propaganda. The reasoning is that the challenge is as much about making their societies more resilient as it is about Putin's posturing. With that logic, it hardly even matters whether or not Putin is actually pulling strings in the US campaign – the fact that he is widely perceived to be doing so is a victory in itself.

Likewise, when public confidence in western institutions is eroded (the suspicion that elections can be rigged, or that elites always lie and plot against the people), one clear beneficiary is the man who sits in the Kremlin. Russian propaganda is more effective if democracy is seen as tainted and perverted everywhere.

This is not to say that the rope Lenin mentioned is at the ready. In fact, Putin's strategy might actually be backfiring. Russia's actions and antics have arguably done more for Ukrainian national self-awareness, Baltic security efforts and Nato's renewed sense of mission (territorial defence in Europe) than any other development since the break-up of the Soviet Union. What remains to be seen is whether loss of confidence within the west, over the very functioning of liberal democracy, threatens to encourage Putin's worst instincts. That perhaps is worth pondering, before we dismiss MI5's warnings as needlessly alarming, or even unjustified.

==

The tainted election. Russia's Hand in America's Election

Paul Krugman New York Times, Dec. 12, 2016

The C.I.A., according to The Washington Post, has now determined that hackers working for the Russian government worked to tilt the 2016 election to Donald Trump. This has actually been obvious for months, but the agency was reluctant to state that conclusion before the election out of fear that it would be seen as taking a political role.
Meanwhile, the F.B.I. went public 10 days before the election, dominating headlines and TV coverage across the country with a letter strongly implying that it might be about to find damning new evidence against Hillary Clinton — when it turned out, literally, to have found nothing at all.

Did the combination of Russian and F.B.I. intervention swing the election? Yes. Mrs. Clinton lost three states – Michigan, Wisconsin, and Pennsylvania – by less than a percentage point, and Florida by only slightly more. If she had won any three of those states, she would be president-elect. Is there any reasonable doubt that Putin/Comey made the difference?

And it wouldn't have been seen as a marginal victory, either. Even as it was, Mrs. Clinton received almost three million more votes than her opponent, giving her a popular margin close to that of George W. Bush in 2004.

So this was a tainted election. It was not, as far as we can tell, stolen in the sense that votes were counted wrong, and the result won't be overturned. But the result was nonetheless illegitimate in important ways; the victor was rejected by the public, and won the Electoral College only thanks to foreign intervention and grotesquely inappropriate, partisan behaviour on the part of domestic law enforcement.

==

There's a smell of treason in the air
Nicholas Kristof , 23 March 2017   The New York Times

The greatest political scandal in American history was not Aaron Burr's shooting of Alexander Hamilton, and perhaps wasn't even Watergate. Rather it may have been Richard Nixon's secret efforts in 1968 to sabotage a U.S. diplomatic effort to end the Vietnam War.

Nixon's initiative, long rumored but confirmed only a few months ago, was meant to improve his election chances that year. After Nixon won, the war dragged on and cost thousands of additional American and Vietnamese lives; it's hard to see his behavior as anything but treason.

Now the F.B.I. confirms that we have had an investigation underway for eight months into whether another presidential campaign colluded with a foreign power so as to win an election. To me, that, too, would amount to treason.

I've been speaking to intelligence experts, Americans and foreigners alike, and they mostly (but not entirely) believe there was a Trump-Russia cooperation of some kind. But this is uncertain; it's prudent to note that James Clapper, the intelligence director under Barack Obama, said that as of January he had seen no evidence of collusion but that he favors an investigation to get to the bottom of it.

I'm also told (not by a Democrat!) that there's a persuasive piece of intelligence on ties between Russia and a member of the Trump team that isn't yet public.

The most likely scenario for collusion seems fuzzier and less transactional than many Democrats anticipate. A bit of conjecture:

The Russians for years had influence over Donald Trump because of their investments with him, and he was by nature inclined to admire Vladimir Putin as a strongman ruler. Meanwhile, Trump had in his orbit a number of people with Moscow ties, including Paul Manafort, who practically bleeds borscht.

The Associated Press reports that Manafort had secretly worked for a Russian billionaire close to Putin, signing a $10-million-a-year contract in 2006 to promote the interests of the Putin government. The arrangement lasted at least until 2009.

As The A.P. puts it, Manafort offered to "influence politics, business dealings and news coverage inside the United States, Europe and the former Soviet republics to benefit the Putin government." (Manafort told The A.P. that his work was being falsely portrayed as nefarious.)

This is guesswork, but it might have seemed natural for Trump aides to try to milk Russian contacts for useful information about the Clinton campaign. Likewise, the Russians despised Hillary Clinton and would have been interested in milking American contacts for information about how best to damage her chances.

At some point, I suspect, members of the Trump team gained knowledge of Russian hacking into Clinton emails, which would explain why Trump friend Roger Stone tweeted things like "Trust me, it will soon the Podesta's time in the barrel."

This kind of soft collusion, evolving over the course of the campaign without a clear quid pro quo, might also explain why there weren't greater efforts to hide the Trump team's ties to Russia, or to camouflage its softening of the Republican Party platform position toward Moscow.

One crucial unknown: Did Russia try to funnel money into Trump's campaign coffers? In European elections, Russia has regularly tried to influence results by providing secret funds. I'm sure the F.B.I. is looking into whether there were suspicious financial transfers.

The contacts with Russia are by Trump's aides, and the challenge will be to connect any collusion to the president himself. The White House is already distancing itself from Manafort, claiming that he played only a "very limited role" in the campaign — even though he was Trump's campaign chairman!

Many Democrats are, I think, too focused on Jeff Sessions and have too transactional a view of what may have unfolded. Treason isn't necessarily spelled out as a quid pro quo, and it wasn't when Nixon tried to sink the Vietnam peace initiative in 1968.

In the past, as when foreign funds made their way into Bill Clinton's 1996 re-election campaign, Republicans showed intense interest in foreign interference in the political process. So it's sad to see some Republicans (I mean you, Devin Nunes!) trying to hijack today's House investigation to make it about leaks.

Really? Our country was attacked by Russia, and you're obsessed with leaks? Do you honestly think that the culprit in Watergate wasn't Nixon but the famed leaker Deep Throat? Republicans should replace Nunes as head of the House Intelligence Committee; he can't simultaneously be Trump's advocate and his investigator.

The fundamental question now isn't about Trump's lies, or intelligence leaks, or inadvertent collection of Trump communications. Rather, the crucial question is as monumental as it is simple: Was there treason?

We don't know yet what unfolded, and raw intelligence is often wrong. But the issue cries out for a careful, public and bipartisan investigation by an independent commission.

"There's a smell of treason in the air," Douglas Brinkley, the historian, told The Washington Post. He's right, and we must dispel that stench.

===
It's not all Putin's fault, my note 18 December 2014

As Dostoyevsky said - we are all guilty. Guilty of perverse and incompetent diplomacy. That includes President Obama who couldn't control his neo-conservatives, President Putin who failed to check his perfectly legitimate fear of American hegemony. And the EU – also incompetent with no ability to form foreign policy and resist that American neo-conservative aggression. And the Murdoch dominated world media, perversely persuading the 'West' that 'it's all Putin's fault'.

RUSSIA & THE US, PUTIN: PUTIN'S ACTION IN FAVOUR OF DONALD TRUMP

Sergey Lavrov's article "Russia's Foreign Policy : Historical Background" for "Russia in Global Affairs" magazine, 3 March, 2016

International relations have entered a very difficult period, and Russia once again finds itself at the crossroads of key trends that determine the vector of future global development.

Many different opinions have been expressed in this connection including the fear that we have a distorted view of the international situation and Russia's international standing. I perceive this as an echo of the eternal dispute between pro-Western liberals and the advocates of Russia's unique path. There are also those, both in Russia and outside of it, who believe that Russia is doomed to drag behind, trying to catch up with the West and forced to bend to other players' rules, and hence will be unable to claim its rightful place in international affairs. I'd like to use this opportunity to express some of my views and to back them with examples from history and historical parallels.

It is an established fact that a substantiated policy is impossible without reliance on history. This reference to history is absolutely justified, especially considering recent celebrations. In 2015, we celebrated the 70th anniversary of Victory in WWII, and in 2014, we marked a century since the start of WWI. In 2012, we marked 200 years of the Battle of Borodino and 400 years of Moscow's liberation from the Polish invaders. If we look at these events carefully, we'll see that they clearly point to Russia's special role in European and global history.

History doesn't confirm the widespread belief that Russia has always camped in Europe's backyard and has been Europe's political outsider. I'd like to remind you that the adoption of Christianity in Russia in 988 – we marked 1025 years of that event quite recently – boosted the development of state institutions, social relations and culture and eventually made Kievan Rus a full member of the European community. At that time, dynastic marriages were the best gauge of a country's role in the system of international relations. In the 11th century, three daughters of Grand Prince Yaroslav the Wise became the queens of Norway and Denmark, Hungary and France. Yaroslav's sister married the Polish king and granddaughter the German emperor.

Numerous scientific investigations bear witness to the high cultural and spiritual level of Rus of those days, a level that was frequently higher than in western European states. Many prominent Western thinkers recognized that Rus was part of the European context. At the same time, Russian people possessed a cultural matrix of their own and an original type of spirituality and never merged with the West. It is instructive to recall in this connection what was for my people a tragic and in many respects critical epoch of the Mongolian invasion. The great Russian poet and writer Alexander Pushkin wrote: "The barbarians did not dare to leave an enslaved Rus in their rear and returned to their Eastern steppes. Christian enlightenment was saved by a ravaged and dying Russia." We also know an alternative view offered by prominent historian and ethnologist Lev Gumilyov, who believed that the Mongolian invasion had prompted the emergence of a new Russian ethnos and that the Great Steppe had given us an additional impetus for development.

However that may be, it is clear that the said period was extremely important for the assertion of the Russian State's independent role in Eurasia. Let us recall in this connection the policy pursued by Grand Prince Alexander Nevsky, who opted to temporarily submit to Golden Horde rulers, who were tolerant of Christianity, in order to uphold the Russians' right to have a faith of their own and to decide their fate, despite the European West's attempts to put Russian lands under full control and to deprive Russians of their identity. I am confident that this wise and forward-looking policy is in our genes.

Rus bent under but was not broken by the heavy Mongolian yoke, and managed to emerge from this dire trial as a single state, which was later regarded by both the West and the East as the successor to the Byzantine Empire that ceased to exist in 1453. An imposing country stretching along what was practically the entire eastern perimeter of Europe, Russia began a natural expansion towards the Urals and Siberia, absorbing their huge territories. Already then it was a powerful balancing factor in European political combinations, including the well-known Thirty Years' War that gave birth to the Westphalian system of international relations, whose principles, primarily respect for state sovereignty, are of importance even today.

At this point we are approaching a dilemma that has been evident for several centuries. While the rapidly developing Moscow state naturally played an increasing role in European affairs, the European countries had apprehensions about the nascent giant in the East and tried to isolate it whenever possible and prevent it from taking part in Europe's most important affairs.

The seeming contradiction between the traditional social order and a striving for modernisation based on the most [*words missing*]

113

traditions. This is all the more typical of Russia that is essentially a branch of European civilisation.

Incidentally, the need for modernisation based on European achievements was clearly manifest in Russian society under Tsar Alexis, while talented and ambitious Peter the Great gave it a strong boost. Relying on tough domestic measures and resolute, and successful, foreign policy, Peter the Great managed to put Russia into the category of Europe's leading countries in a little over two decades. Since that time Russia's position could no longer be ignored. Not a single European issue can be resolved without Russia's opinion.

It wouldn't be accurate to assume that everyone was happy about this state of affairs. Repeated attempts to return this country into the pre-Peter times were made over subsequent centuries but failed. In the middle 18th century Russia played a key role in a pan-European conflict – the Seven Years' War. At that time, Russian troops made a triumphal entry into Berlin, the capital of Prussia under Frederick II who had a reputation for invincibility. Prussia was saved from an inevitable rout only because Empress Elizabeth died a sudden death and was succeeded by Peter III who sympathised with Frederick II. This turn in German history is still referred to as the Miracle of the House of Brandenburg. Russia's size, power and influence grew substantially under Catherine the Great when, as then Chancellor Alexander Bezborodko put it, "Not a single cannon in Europe could be fired without our consent."

I'd like to quote the opinion of a reputable researcher of Russian history, Hélène Carrère d'Encausse, the permanent secretary of the French Academy. She said the Russian Empire was the greatest empire of all times in the totality of all parameters – its size, an ability to administer its territories and the longevity of its existence. Following Russian philosopher Nikolai Berdyayev, she insists that history has imbued Russia with the mission of being a link between the East and the West.

During at least the past two centuries any attempts to unite Europe without Russia and against it have inevitably led to grim tragedies, the consequences of which were always overcome with the decisive participation of our country. I'm referring, in part, to the Napoleonic wars upon the completion of which Russia rescued the system of international relations that was based on the balance of forces and mutual consideration for national interests and ruled out the total dominance of one state in Europe. We remember that Emperor Alexander I took an active role in the drafting of decisions of the 1815 Vienna Congress that ensured the development of Europe without serious armed clashes during the subsequent 40 years.

Incidentally, to a certain extent the ideas of Alexander I could be described as a prototype of the concept on subordinating national interests to common goals, primarily, the maintenance of peace and order in Europe. As the Russian emperor said, "there can be no more English, French, Russian or Austrian policy. There can be only one policy – a common policy that must be accepted by both peoples and sovereigns for common happiness."

By the same token, the Vienna system was destroyed in the wake of the desire to marginalise Russia in European affairs. Paris was obsessed with this idea during the reign of Emperor Napoleon III. In his attempt to forge an anti-Russian alliance, the French monarch was willing, as a hapless chess grandmaster, to sacrifice all the other figures. How did it play out? Indeed, Russia was defeated in the Crimean War of 1853-1856, the consequences of which it managed to overcome soon due to a consistent and far-sighted policy pursued by Chancellor Alexander Gorchakov. As for Napoleon III, he ended his rule in German captivity, and the nightmare of the Franco-German confrontation loomed over Western Europe for decades.

Here is another Crimean War-related episode. As we know, the Austrian Emperor refused to help Russia, which, a few years earlier, in 1849, had come to his help during the Hungarian revolt. Then Austrian Foreign Minister Felix Schwarzenberg famously said: "Europe would be astonished by the extent of Austria's ingratitude." In general, the imbalance of pan-European mechanisms triggered a chain of events that led to the First World War.

Notably, back then Russian diplomacy also advanced ideas that were ahead of their time. The Hague Peace conferences of 1899 and 1907, convened at the initiative of Emperor Nicholas II, were the first attempts to agree on curbing the arms race and stopping preparations for a devastating war. But not many people know about it.

The First World War claimed lives and caused the suffering of countless millions of people and led to the collapse of four empires. In this connection, it is appropriate to recall yet another anniversary, which will be marked next year – the 100th anniversary of the Russian Revolution. Today we are faced with the need to develop a balanced and objective assessment of those events, especially in an environment where, particularly in the West, many are willing to use this date to mount even more information attacks on Russia, and to portray the 1917 Revolution as a barbaric coup that dragged down all of European history. Even worse, they want to equate the Soviet regime to Nazism, and partially blame it for starting WWII.

Without a doubt, the Revolution of 1917 and the ensuing Civil War were a terrible tragedy for our nation. However, all other revolutions were tragic as well. This does not prevent our French colleagues from extolling their upheaval, which, in addition to the slogans of liberty, equality and fraternity, also involved the use of the guillotine, and rivers of blood.

Undoubtedly, the Russian Revolution was a major event which impacted world history in many controversial ways. It has become regarded as a kind of experiment in implementing socialist ideas, which were then widely spread across Europe. The people supported them, because wide masses gravitated towards social organisation with reliance on the collective and community principles.

Serious researchers clearly see the impact of reforms in the Soviet Union on the formation of the so-called welfare state in Western Europe in the post-WWII period. European governments decided to introduce unprecedented measures of social protection under the influence of the example of the Soviet Union in an effort to cut the ground from under the feet of the left-wing political forces.

One can say that the 40 years following World War II were a surprisingly good time for Western Europe, which was spared the need to make its own major decisions under the umbrella of the US-Soviet confrontation and enjoyed unique opportunities for steady development.

In these circumstances, Western European countries have implemented several ideas regarding conversion of the capitalist and socialist models, which, as a preferred form of socioeconomic progress, were promoted by Pitirim Sorokin and other outstanding thinkers of the 20th century. Over the past 20 years, we have been witnessing the reverse process in Europe and the United States: the reduction of the middle class, increased social inequality, and the dismantling of controls over big business.

The role which the Soviet Union played in decolonisation, and promoting international relations principles, such as the independent development of nations and their right to self-determination, is undeniable.

I will not dwell on the points related to Europe slipping into WWII. Clearly, the anti-Russian aspirations of the European elites, and their desire to unleash Hitler's war machine on the Soviet Union played their fatal part here. Redressing the situation after this terrible disaster involved the participation of our country as a key partner in determining the parameters of the European and the world order.

In this context, the notion of the "clash of two totalitarianisms," which is now actively inculcated in European minds, including at schools, is groundless and immoral. The Soviet Union, for all its evils, never aimed to destroy entire nations. Winston Churchill, who all his life was a principled opponent of the Soviet Union and played a major role in going from the WWII alliance to a new confrontation with the Soviet Union, said that graciousness, i.e. life in accordance with conscience, is the Russian way of doing things.

If you take an unbiased look at the smaller European countries, which previously were part of the Warsaw Treaty, and are now members of the EU or NATO, it is clear that the issue was not about going from subjugation to freedom, which Western masterminds like to talk about, but rather a change of leadership.Russian President Vladimir Putin spoke about it not long ago. The representatives of these countries concede behind closed doors that they can't take any significant decision without the green light from Washington or Brussels.

It seems that in the context of the 100th anniversary of the Russian Revolution, it is important for us to understand the continuity of Russian history, which should include all of its periods without exception, and the importance of the synthesis of all the positive traditions and historical experience as the basis for making dynamic advances and upholding the rightful role of our country as a leading centre of the modern world, and a provider of the values of sustainable development, security and stability.

The post-war world order relied on confrontation between two world systems and was far from ideal, yet it was sufficient to preserve international peace and to avoid the worst possible temptation – the use of weapons of mass destruction, primarily nuclear weapons. There is no substance behind the popular belief that the Soviet Union's dissolution signified Western victory in the Cold War. It was the result of our people's will for change plus an unlucky chain of events.

These developments resulted in a truly tectonic shift in the international landscape. In fact, they changed global politics altogether, considering that the end of the Cold War and related ideological confrontation offered a unique opportunity to change the

European architecture on the principles of indivisible and equal security and broad cooperation without dividing lines.

We had a practical chance to mend Europe's divide and implement the dream of a common European home, which many European thinkers and politicians, including President Charles de Gaulle of France, wholeheartedly embraced. Russia was fully open to this option and advanced many proposals and initiatives in this connection. Logically, we should have created a new foundation for European security by strengthening the military and political components of the Organisation for Security and Cooperation in Europe (OSCE). Vladimir Putin said in a recent interview with the German newspaper Bild that German politician Egon Bahr proposed similar approaches.

Unfortunately, our Western partners chose differently. They opted to expand NATO eastward and to advance the geopolitical space they controlled closer to the Russian border. This is the essence of the systemic problems that have soured Russia's relations with the United States and the European Union. It is notable that George Kennan, the architect of the US policy of containment of the Soviet Union, said in his winter years that the ratification of NATO expansion was "a tragic mistake."

The underlying problem of this Western policy is that it disregarded the global context. The current globalised world is based on an unprecedented interconnection between countries, and so it's impossible to develop relations between Russia and the EU as if they remained at the core of global politics as during the Cold War. We must take note of the powerful processes that are underway in Asia Pacific, the Middle East, Africa and Latin America.

Rapid changes in all areas of international life is the primary sign of the current stage. Indicatively, they often take an unexpected turn. Thus, the concept of "the end of history" developed by well-known US sociologist and political researcher Francis Fukuyama, that was popular in the 1990s, has become clearly inconsistent today. According to this concept, rapid globalisation signals the ultimate victory of the liberal capitalist model, whereas all other models should adapt to it under the guidance of the wise Western teachers.

In reality, the second wave of globalisation (the first occurred before World War I) led to the dispersal of global economic might and, hence, of political influence, and to the emergence of new and large centres of power, primarily in the Asia-Pacific Region. China's rapid upsurge is the clearest example. Owing to unprecedented economic growth rates, in just three decades it became the second and, calculated as per purchasing power parity, the first economy in the world. This example illustrates an axiomatic fact – there are many development models– which rules out the monotony of existence within the uniform, Western frame of reference.

Consequently, there has been a relative reduction in the influence of the so-called "historical West" that was used to seeing itself as the master of the human race's destinies for almost five centuries. The competition on the shaping of the world order in the 21st century has toughened. The transition from the Cold War to a new international system proved to be much longer and more painful than it seemed 20-25 years ago.

Against this backdrop, one of the basic issues in international affairs is the form that is being acquired by this generally natural competition between the world's leading powers. We see how the United States and the US-led Western alliance are trying to preserve their dominant positions by any available method or, to use the American lexicon, ensure their "global leadership". Many diverse ways of exerting pressure, economic sanctions and even direct armed intervention are being used. Large-scale information wars are being waged. Technology of unconstitutional change of governments by launching "colour" revolutions has been tried and tested. Importantly, democratic revolutions appear to be destructive for the nations targeted by such actions. Our country that went through a historical period of encouraging artificial transformations abroad, firmly proceeds from the preference of evolutionary changes that should be carried out in the forms and at a speed that conform to the traditions of a society and its level of development.

Western propaganda habitually accuses Russia of "revisionism," and the alleged desire to destroy the established international system, as if it was us who bombed Yugoslavia in 1999 in violation of the UN Charter and the Helsinki Final Act, as if it was Russia that ignored international law by invading Iraq in 2003 and distorted UN Security Council resolutions by overthrowing Muammar Gaddafi's regime by force in Libya in 2011. There are many examples.

This discourse about "revisionism" does not hold water. It is based on the simple and even primitive logic that only Washington can set the tune in world affairs. In line with this logic, the principle once formulated by George Orwell and moved to the international level, sounds like the following: all states are equal but some states are more equal than others. However, today international relations are too sophisticated a mechanism to be controlled from one centre. This is obvious given the results of US interference: There is virtually no state in Libya; Iraq is balancing on the brink of disintegration, and so on and so forth.

A reliable solution to the problems of the modern world can only be achieved through serious and honest cooperation between the leading states and their associations in order to address common challenges. Such an interaction should include all the colours of the modern world, and be based on its cultural and civilisational diversity, as well as reflect the interests of the international community's key components.

We know from experience that when these principles are applied in practice, it is possible to achieve specific and tangible results, such as the agreement on the Iranian nuclear programme, the elimination of Syrian chemical weapons, the agreement on stopping hostilities in Syria, and the development of the basic parameters of the global climate agreement. This shows the need to restore the culture of compromise, the reliance on the diplomatic work, which can be difficult, even exhausting, but which remains, in essence, the only way to ensure a mutually acceptable solution to problems by peaceful means.

Our approaches are shared by most countries of the world, including our Chinese partners, other BRICS and SCO nations, and our friends in the EAEU, the CSTO, and the CIS. In other words, we can say that Russia is fighting not against someone, but for the resolution of all the issues on an equal and mutually respectful basis, which alone can serve as a reliable foundation for a long-term improvement of international relations.

Our most important task is to join our efforts against not some far-fetched, but very real challenges, among which the terrorist aggression is the most pressing one. The extremists from ISIS, Jabhat an-Nusra and the like managed for the first time to establish control over large territories in Syria and Iraq. They are trying to extend their influence to other countries and regions, and are committing acts of terrorism around the world. Underestimating this risk is nothing short of criminal shortsightedness.

The Russian President called for forming a broad-based front in order to defeat the terrorists militarily. The Russian Aerospace Forces make an important contribution to this effort. At the same time, we are working hard to establish collective actions regarding the political settlement of the conflicts in this crisis-ridden region.

Importantly, the long-term success can only be achieved on the basis of movement to the partnership of civilisations based on respectful interaction of diverse cultures and religions. We believe that human solidarity must have a moral basis formed by traditional values that are largely shared by the world's leading religions. In this connection, I would like to draw your attention to the joint statement by Patriarch Kirill and Pope Francis, in which, among other things, they have expressed support for the family as a natural centre of life of individuals and society.

I repeat, we are not seeking confrontation with the United States, or the European Union, or NATO. On the contrary, Russia is open to the widest possible cooperation with its Western partners. We continue to believe that the best way to ensure the interests of the peoples living in Europe is to form a common economic and humanitarian space from the Atlantic to the Pacific, so that the newly formed Eurasian Economic Union could be an integrating link between Europe and Asia Pacific. We strive to do our best to overcome obstacles on that way, including the settlement of the Ukraine crisis caused by the coup in Kiev in February 2014, on the basis of the Minsk Agreements.

I'd like to quote wise and politically experienced Henry Kissinger, who, speaking recently in Moscow, said that "Russia should be perceived as an essential element of any new global equilibrium, not primarily as a threat to the United States... I am here to argue for the possibility of a dialogue that seeks to merge our futures rather than elaborate our conflicts. This requires respect by both sides of the vital values and interest of the other." We share such an approach. And we will continue to defend the principles of law and justice in international affairs.

Speaking about Russia's role in the world as a great power, Russian philosopher Ivan Ilyin said that the greatness of a country is not determined by the size of its territory or the number of its inhabitants, but by the capacity of its people and its government to take on the burden of great world problems and to deal with these problems in a creative manner. A great power is the one which, asserting its existence and its interest ... introduces a creative and meaningful legal idea to the entire assembly of the nations, the entire "concert" of the peoples and states. It is difficult to disagree with these words.

===

President Putin's speech 2 October, 2007 at the NATO Munich Security Conference

[I would like to know if any politician or media has so much as mentioned this important speech by Vladimir PUTIN since the Georgia affair. I personally have not seen any mention of it since it was given on 2 October 2007 to the Munich Security Conference: - and harshly criticised as anti-American tirade!

For me, and for some others studying Russian foreign policy, it bears the hallmarks of having been prepared by Russia's remarkable pro-European foreign minister Sergey Lavrov. One expert rather facetiously described him as Putin's Chou En-lai who was the reasonable face of Mao Tse Tung!

Rebuffed by the West Putin became obsessed with American neo-conservatism and its unipolar aims. Everywhere he sees some American threat even where there is none – this gave him the excuse to grab ever more power - a dangerous and unprincipled quasi-dictator].

Dear ladies and gentlemen!

The potential danger of the destabilisation of international relations is connected with obvious stagnation in the disarmament issue.

Russia supports the renewal of dialogue on this important question.

It is important to conserve the international legal framework relating to weapons destruction and therefore ensure continuity in the process of reducing nuclear weapons.

Together with the United States of America we agreed to reduce our nuclear strategic missile capabilities to up to 1700-2000 nuclear warheads by 31 December 2012. Russia intends to strictly fulfil the obligations it has taken on. We hope that our partners will also act in a transparent way and will refrain from laying aside a couple of hundred superfluous nuclear warheads for a rainy day.

And if today the new American Defence Minister declares that the United States will not hide these superfluous weapons in warehouse or, as one might say, under a pillow or under the blanket, then I suggest that we all rise and greet this declaration standing. It would be a very important declaration.

Russia strictly adheres to and intends to further adhere to the Treaty on the Non-Proliferation of Nuclear Weapons as well as the multilateral supervision regime for missile technologies. The principles incorporated in these documents are universal ones.

In connection with this I would like to recall that in the 1980s the USSR and the United States signed an agreement on destroying a whole range of small- and medium-range missiles but these documents do not have a universal character.

Today many other countries have these missiles, including the Democratic People's Republic of Korea, the Republic of Korea, India, Iran, Pakistan and Israel. Many countries are working on these systems and plan to incorporate them as part of their weapons arsenals. And only the United States and Russia bear the responsibility to not create such weapons systems.

It is obvious that in these conditions we must think about ensuring our own security.
At the same time, it is impossible to sanction the appearance of new, destabilising high-tech weapons. Needless to say it refers to measures to prevent a new area of confrontation, especially in outer space. Star wars is no longer a fantasy – it is a reality. In the middle of the 1980s

our American partners were already able to intercept their own satellite.

In Russia's opinion, the militarisation of outer space could have unpredictable consequences for the international community, and provoke nothing less than the beginning of a nuclear era. And we have come forward more than once with initiatives designed to prevent the use of weapons in outer space.

Today I would like to tell you that we have prepared a project for an agreement on the prevention of deploying weapons in outer space. And in the near future it will be sent to our partners as an official proposal. Let's work on this together.

Plans to expand certain elements of the anti-missile defence system to Europe cannot help but disturb us. Who needs the next step of what would be, in this case, an inevitable arms race? I deeply doubt that Europeans themselves do.

Missile weapons with a range of about five to eight thousand kilometres that really pose a threat to Europe do not exist in any of the so-called problem countries. And in the near future and prospects, this will not happen and is not even foreseeable. And any hypothetical launch of, for example, a North Korean rocket to American territory through western Europe obviously contradicts the laws of ballistics. As we say in Russia, it would be like using the right hand to reach the left ear.

And here in Germany I cannot help but mention the pitiable condition of the Treaty on Conventional Armed Forces in Europe.

The Adapted Treaty on Conventional Armed Forces in Europe was signed in 1999. It took into account a new geopolitical reality, namely the elimination of the Warsaw bloc. Seven years have passed and only four states have ratified this document, including the Russian Federation.

NATO countries openly declared that they will not ratify this treaty, including the provisions on flank restrictions (on deploying a certain number of armed forces in the flank zones), until Russia removed its military bases from Georgia and Moldova. Our army is leaving Georgia, even according to an accelerated schedule. We resolved the problems we had with our Georgian colleagues, as everybody knows.

There are still 1,500 servicemen in Moldova that are carrying out peacekeeping operations and protecting warehouses with ammunition left over from Soviet times. We constantly discuss this issue with Mr Solana and he knows our position. We are ready to further work in this direction.

But what is happening at the same time? Simultaneously the so-called flexible frontline American bases with up to five thousand men in each. It turns out that NATO has put its frontline forces on our borders, and we continue to strictly fulfil the treaty obligations and do not react to these actions at all.

I think it is obvious that NATO expansion does not have any relation with the modernisation of the Alliance itself or with ensuring security in Europe. On the contrary, it represents a serious provocation that reduces the level of mutual trust. And we have the right to ask: against whom is this expansion intended? And what happened to the assurances our western partners made after the dissolution of the Warsaw Pact? Where are those declarations today? No one even remembers them.

But I will allow myself to remind this audience what was said. I would like to quote the speech of NATO General Secretary Mr Woerner in Brussels on 17 May 1990. He said at the time that: "the fact that we are ready not to place a NATO army outside of German territory gives the Soviet Union a firm security guarantee". Where are these guarantees?

The stones and concrete blocks of the Berlin Wall have long been distributed as souvenirs. But we should not forget that the fall of the Berlin Wall was possible thanks to a historic choice – one that was also made by our people, the people of Russia – a choice in favour of democracy, freedom, openness and a sincere partnership with all the members of the big European family.

And now they are trying to impose new dividing lines and walls on us – these walls may be virtual but they are nevertheless dividing, ones that cut through our continent. And is it possible that we will once again require many years and decades, as well as several generations of politicians, to dissemble and dismantle these new walls?

Dear ladies and gentlemen!

We are unequivocally in favour of strengthening the regime of non-proliferation. The present international legal principles allow us to develop technologies to manufacture nuclear fuel for peaceful purposes. And many countries with all good reasons want to create their own nuclear energy as a basis for their energy independence. But we also understand that these technologies can be quickly transformed into nuclear weapons.

This creates serious international tensions. The situation surrounding the Iranian nuclear programme acts as a clear example. And if the international community does not find a reasonable solution for resolving this conflict of interests, the world will continue to suffer similar, destabilising crises because there are more threshold countries than simply Iran. We both know this. We are going to constantly fight against the threat of the proliferation of weapons of mass destruction.

Last year Russia put forward the initiative to establish international centres for the enrichment of uranium. We are open to the possibility that such centres not only be created in Russia, but also in other countries where there is a legitimate basis for using civil nuclear energy. Countries that want to develop their nuclear energy could guarantee that they will receive fuel through direct participation in these centres. And the centres would, of course, operate under strict IAEA supervision.

The latest initiatives put forward by American President George W. Bush are in conformity with the Russian proposals. I consider that Russia and the USA are objectively and equally interested in strengthening the regime of the non-proliferation of weapons of mass destruction and their deployment. It is precisely our countries, with leading nuclear and missile capabilities, that must act as leaders in developing new, stricter non-proliferation measures. Russia is ready for such work. We are engaged in consultations with our American friends.

In general, we should talk about establishing a whole system of political incentives and economic stimuli whereby it would not be in states' interests to establish their own capabilities in the nuclear fuel cycle but they would still have the opportunity to develop nuclear energy and strengthen their energy capabilities.

In connection with this I shall talk about international energy cooperation in more detail. Madam Federal Chancellor also spoke about this briefly – she mentioned, touched on this theme. In the energy sector Russia intends to create uniform market principles and transparent conditions for all. It is obvious that energy prices must be determined by the market instead of being the subject of political speculation, economic pressure or blackmail.

We are open to cooperation. Foreign companies participate in all our major energy projects. According to different estimates, up to 26 percent of the oil extraction in Russia – and please think about this figure – up to 26 percent of the oil extraction in Russia is done by foreign capital. Try, try to find me a similar example where Russian business participates extensively in key economic sectors in western countries. Such examples do not exist! There are no such examples.

I would also recall the parity of foreign investments in Russia and those Russia makes abroad. The parity is about fifteen to one. And here you have an obvious example of the openness and stability of the Russian economy.

Economic security is the sector in which all must adhere to uniform principles. We are ready to compete fairly.

For that reason more and more opportunities are appearing in the Russian economy. Experts and our western partners are objectively evaluating these changes. As such, Russia's OECD sovereign credit rating improved and Russia passed from the fourth to the third group. And today in Munich I would like to use this occasion to thank our German colleagues for their help in the above decision.

Furthermore. As you know, the process of Russia joining the WTO has reached its final stages. I would point out that during long, difficult talks we heard words about freedom of speech, free trade, and equal possibilities more than once but, for some reason, exclusively in reference to the Russian market.

And there is still one more important theme that directly affects global security.

Today many talk about the struggle against poverty. What is actually happening in this sphere? On the one hand, financial resources are allocated for programmes to help the world's poorest countries – and at times substantial financial resources. But to be honest -- and many here also know this – linked with the development of that same donor country's companies. And on the other hand, developed countries simultaneously keep their agricultural subsidies and limit some countries' access to high-tech products.

And let's say things as they are – one hand distributes charitable help and the other hand not only preserves economic backwardness but also reaps the profits thereof. The increasing social tension in depressed regions inevitably results in the growth of radicalism, extremism, feeds terrorism and local conflicts. And if all this happens in, shall we say, a region such as the Middle East where there is increasingly the sense that the world at large is unfair, then there is the risk of global destabilisation.

It is obvious that the world's leading countries should see this threat. And that they should therefore build a more democratic, fairer system of global economic relations, a system that would give everyone the chance and the possibility to develop.

Dear ladies and gentlemen, speaking at the Conference on Security Policy, it is impossible not to mention the activities of the Organisation for Security and Cooperation in Europe (OSCE). As is well-known, this organisation was created to examine all – I shall emphasise this – all aspects of security: military, political, economic, humanitarian and, especially, the relations between these spheres.

What do we see happening today? We see that this balance is clearly destroyed.
People are trying to transform the OSCE into a vulgar instrument designed to promote the foreign policy interests of one or a group of countries. And this task is also being accomplished by the OSCE's

bureaucratic apparatus which is absolutely not connected with the state founders in any way. Decision-making procedures and the involvement of so-called non-governmental organisations are tailored for this task. These organisations are formally independent but they are purposefully financed and therefore under control.

According to the founding documents, in the humanitarian sphere the OSCE is designed to assist country members in observing international human rights norms at their request. This is an important task. We support this. But this does not mean interfering in the internal affairs of other countries, and especially not imposing a regime that determines how these states should live and develop.

It is obvious that such interference does not promote the development of democratic states at all. On the contrary, it makes them dependent and, as a consequence, politically and economically unstable.
We expect that the OSCE be guided by its primary tasks and build relations with sovereign states based on respect, trust and transparency.

Dear ladies and gentlemen!

In conclusion I would like to note the following. We very often – and personally, I very often – hear appeals by our partners, including our European partners, to the effect that Russia should play an increasingly active role in world affairs.

In connection with this I would allow myself to make one small remark. It is hardly necessary to incite us to do so. Russia is a country with a history that spans more than a thousand years and has practically always used the privilege to carry out an independent foreign policy.

We are not going to change this tradition today. At the same time, we are well aware of how the world has changed and we have a realistic sense of our own opportunities and potential. And of course we would like to interact with responsible and independent partners with whom we could work together in constructing a fair and democratic world order that would ensure security and prosperity not only for a select few, but for all.

Thank you for your attention.

Chistopher Steele's Frustration, The Independent 13 January 2017

[Former MI6 agent Christopher Steele's frustration as the FBI sat on his Donald Trump Russia file for months. Steele was so concerned by its revelations that he worked without payment after Trump's election victory in November 2016]

Kim Sengupta Defence Editor
13 January 2017

Christopher Steele, the former MI6 spy who prepared the explosive <u>Trump</u> report, has been approached about testifying before the US Senate Intelligence Committee's investigation into the new President's alleged links with <u>Russia</u>, *The Independent* can reveal.

Mr Steele's friends say it is currently unlikely he would be willing to travel to the US. But it is understood Democrats – as well as some Republicans – in Congress are prepared to facilitate discreet initial meetings in the UK or on other neutral territory.

John McCain, the former Republican presidential candidate, and chairman of the Senate Armed Services Committee, sent an intermediary to London in November last year to collect <u>Mr Steele's dossier</u>, which was subsequently passed personally by the Senator to FBI director James Comey.

And Mr Steele had, while carrying out <u>his Trump inquiry</u>, himself liaised for regular periods with the bureau.

Mr Trump has personally attacked Mr Steele, declaring the report on the Kremlin connection by the <u>former MI6 officer</u> as a fabricated work, put together by a "failed spy".

In reality, Mr Steele was, and continues to be, held in high regard by British security and intelligence services as well as the American security officials who worked with him in the past.

It emerged this week that the FBI had, at one stage, proposed to pay him to continue his investigation into Mr Trump and his associates.

Trump denies his team had contact with Russia during election campaign.

But that deal fell through and Mr Steele ultimately continued to work without pay because he was so worried by what he was discovering.

Mr Steele has not yet responded to requests to meet with Senate officials – described as informal at this stage – for testimony, which have come over the last fortnight. But friends say he may be willing to speak about his investigation to senators and US officials if certain security conditions are met.

The development comes amid fresh revelations of the Trump administration's interaction with the Russians. It has emerged that Jeff Sessions, the Attorney General, was in contact with Moscow's ambassador to the US during the election campaign.

Mr Trump's national security adviser, Lieutenant General Michael Flynn, was forced to resign after details of similar communications surfaced last month.
It has also emerged that in the last days of Barack Obama's presidency, officials were so worried that the incoming Trump administration would try to suppress or destroy incriminating material that they passed on information to the intelligence agencies and senior figures in Congress.

There is now similar concern that the Trump White House is trying to sabotage the Russia investigations. Democrats have asked for an inquiry into attempts by White House chief of staff, Reince Priebus, to get the FBI to dismiss media reports about members of Mr Trump's coterie contacting Russian officials.

The drive to contact Mr Steele and others, according to those familiar with the issue, is to try and ensure that as much information as possible is gathered by the Senate Intelligence Committee.

The committee is carrying out its own investigation, separate from one being conducted by the FBI, on the Russian links and attempts by the Kremlin to interfere in the American political process. There will, however, be mutual sharing of relevant material

The Washington Post this week reported the plan by the FBI to pay Mr Steele, who was one of MI6's foremost Russia specialists, to continue his inquiries.

The Independent understands that the offer came after the discovery of a campaign of cyber hacking on state electoral systems in September, which led to a public charge against Moscow by the Obama administration.

Mr Steele became involved in the Trump investigation through the Washington-based firm Fusion GPS, which had been hired by Republican opponents of Mr Trump in September 2015.

In June 2016, Mr Steele joined up with the team. In July, Mr Trump won the Republican nomination and the Democrats became new employers of Mr Steele and Fusion GPS. With that contract due to come to an end with the election, the FBI stepped in with its offer of funding.

Mr Steele has been regularly supplying information to the FBI. In June last year, for instance, he produced a memo which went to the bureau stating that Mr Trump's campaign team had agreed to a Russian request to dilute attention on Moscow's intervention in Ukraine.

Four days later Mr Trump stated that he would recognise Moscow's annexation of Crimea: officials involved in his campaign having already asked the Republican party's election platform to remove a pledge for military assistance to the Ukrainian government against separatist rebels in the east of the country.

Mr Steele claimed the Trump campaign was taking this path because it was aware that the Russians were hacking Democratic Party emails. The same day that Mr Trump spoke about Crimea, he called on the Kremlin to hack Hillary Clinton's emails.

However, Mr Steele became increasingly frustrated that the FBI was failing to take action on the intelligence from others as well as him.

He came to believe there was a cover-up, that a cabal within the bureau blocked a thorough inquiry into Mr Trump, focusing instead on the investigation into Hillary Clinton's emails. The MI6 officer's passing of information to the FBI ceased in December last year.

==

FBI Director Comey's months long delay in making use of Steele's intelligence on Russia's interference until, too late, after Trump's election in November 2016. My contemporary note. [See Comey's book 'A Higher Loyalty' which demonstrates his insistence that justice be done though the heavens fall']

FBI Director James Comey was of course wittingly or not, Putin's ally in throwing the election to Trump – see Paul Krugman's article above.

The above article in The Independent suggests that, as Comey had known of Russia's involvement months before the election, he must have been fully aware of the critical support he would give to Trump by his last minute statement renewing the possibility that Hilary Clinton might be guilty of a crime due to the misuse of her personal email.

Certainly this fact alone should be enough to disqualify Comey from leading a comprehensive inquiry into Russian involvement. Inevitably the taint of treason appears to lie over Comey as well as Trump. But in Comey's case far more likely his deep regard for justice led him to seek justice as he saw it no matter what the consequences. *Fiat justitia ruat caelis.* And the heavens have fallen!

It would be very interesting to know what Putin, Murdoch and Comey now think about their respective roles in making Trump President. Comey is, of course, a Republican. He was appointed by President Obama in 2013 as part of Obama's attempts to have a reasonable working relationship with the 'moderates' in the Republican Party. Because he was privy, at least since August 2016, to the mounting intelligence about Trump's relationship with Putin's intelligence service he must have known better than almost anyone that Trump could well be committing treason. So in addition to what everyone knew or could know from television he was exceptionally well-informed about Trump's unstable character making him, as Mrs. Clinton was claiming, clearly totally unsuitable for the presidency. But Christopher Steele's explosive 35 pages became public as Comey must have expected that they would, so making it impossible for him to prevent an enquiry even if he had wanted to. Indeed when he launched his last minute accusations against Mrs. Clinton in October 2016 he must have known that the '35 pages' would leak to the media. Comey's behaviour is at least as enigmatic as Mrs. May's. Trump could hint that he gave him the presidency so they must be buddies, and Mrs. Clinton can claim that he was responsible for her defeat (with more than a little help from Putin). But a man imbued with the ideal of justice certainly cannot be an ally for Trump as he seeks to avoid impeachment.

As for Putin, he preferred Trump to be President and knew perfectly well he would be a disastrous one, but as the '35 pages' show, he was most anxious to keep his 'Special Political Action' operation secret so that Russia could benefit by the removal of US sanctions because of Russian aggression in the Ukraine. He calculated that he would be able to control his blackmail based on Trump's alleged perverted sexual behaviour with prostitutes that he had arranged for this purpose when Trump was on a vist to Russia.

Putin must have assessed that he was taking a big risk and that if his ambitious ploy were discovered Trump would be unable to favour Russia – indeed US/Russia relations could become much worse. Why then did he take this risk? Presumably simply to prevent the election of Mrs. Clinton, no friend of Russia who, as Secretary of State, had at least permitted the neo-conservatives in State and CIA to launch their own Special Political Action in the, for Russia, sacred Ukraine as part of their drive for that Unipolar world.

As for Rupert Murdoch, he went to town with Fox News, his newspapers and his ubiquitous radio network to provide that hard right Republican 'alternative reality' in which Trump both thrived and revelled. But has he gained from the Trump presidency? In the UK he could calculate that he would have more political say in an isolated Britain than one subject to continental pressures – after all he claims to have got two Prime Ministers elected. But in the US what does he gain from the vagaries of a Trump presidency? Maybe he just enjoys being a virtuoso organist with worldwide engagements skilfully pulling out different stops to suit the tastes of his varied audiences - and enjoying the thrill this gives him. My own guess is that he is now 86 and has lost that touch of genius he had when younger. His children are said to have quite other ideas – if so, it is a pity for the world, and for the US and the UK in particular, that he did not hand over to them before that fatal year, 2016.

That leaves us Mrs May. At first sight, to have a fellow Brexiteer as US president looked to be a heaven-sent opportunity to strengthen the prestigious UK/US 'special relationship' as one of Brexit's greatest boons guaranteeing in future years economic and other benefits from across the Atlantic in place of those that the UK previously enjoyed within the EU. Hence her unseemly haste to meet Trump with the plum of a State visit. Not only was that shown to be highly unpopular in the UK uniting criticism of her for the first time, but within hours of her departure from Washington, it became clear that her wooing of the mercurial Trump had guaranteed nothing.

==

Russian hacking coordinated with other actions including deployment of armed forces – my note.

The famous '35 pages' intelligence report below reveals how President Putin skilfully uses both his armed forces and his intelligence services in coordination to achieve spectacular results – whereas the United States, relying on massive armament has lost its wars since World War two (the parlous state of Afghanistan and the tenuous 'draw' in Korea certainly do not count as victories). And now President Trump seeks to 'make America great again' by spending an extra 54 billion on its conventional defences while slashing much else! Like Judo, today overwhelming opponents can be achieved by the most advanced non-military techniques as President Putin is demonstrating.

Essential to Putin's policies is cyber hacking of a number of Western targets ranging from finance to the West's democratic elections. Fancy Bear, the super hacker, under its real name was first detected in 2007.

140

It is almost certainly an arm of the GRU, Russia's military intelligence service. That is logical when Putin's strategy depends for success on that intimate coordination between military threats and intelligence operations. Over the years it has become ever more sophisticated. Less is known about Cozy Bear, founded a year later in 2008. Both have over the last few years developed highly sophisticated apps which enable the controller to pin-point close races in democracies and then concentrate efforts of every kind using personal denigration, false news etc. on ensuring victory for the local result or for the candidate that Russia wants to win – or maybe just to to stir up associated discontent, for example instigating a riot or, more subtly division through Facebook and Twitter.

The attacks started in 2008 – first targeting ex USSR countries, the Baltics: Latvia, Lithuania and Estonia and Russia's 'soft tummy' Krgystan and Kazakhstan, then Germany, NATO, the Netherlands and France all before 2015. That begs the question – far more important to Russia than these was a 'Leave' result for the UK referendum in 2016 severely fracturing the EU. At least one Member of Parliament has now formally asked for information about that. The suggestion is that the Russians may have used that targeting app to examine the constituencies where a close vote was forecast, and then to concentrate in them with all the tools available to try to achieve a 'Leave' result. The question is - did the UK even know it may have been targeted, and if it did happen, was Russian interference responsible for influencing the referendum result?

==

THE ORBIS BUSINESS INTELLIGENCE REPORT ON RUSSIAN TAMPERING WITH THE NOVEMBER 2016 US PRESIDENTIAL ELECTION, THE '35' PAGES [as published by Buzzfeed 10.1.17]

The report of Trump campaign connections with Russia by Orbis Business Intelligence company. Prepared by Chistopher Steele its Director, a former officer of the UK's Secret Intelligence Service known as MI6. Its information formed a considerable portion of the 17 US intelligence services document that was handed both to then President Barak Obama and then President Elect Donald Trump in December 2016.

It is often referred to as 'The 35 pages' or by sceptics as the 'Dodgy Dossier'. The 17 US intelligence services regarded it as of sufficient importance submit both to then President Obama and President Elect Trump in December 2016.

CONFIDENTIAL/SENSITIVE SOURCE

COMPANY INTELLIGENCE REPORT 2016/080

US PRESIDENTIAL ELECTION: REPUBLICAN CANDIDATE DONALD TRUMP'S ACTIVITIES IN RUSSIA AND COMPROMISING RELATIONSHIP WITH THE KREMLIN

Summary

- Russian regime has been cultivating, supporting and assisting TRUMP for at least 5 years. Aim, endorsed by PUTIN, has been to encourage splits and divisions in western alliance

- So far TRUMP has declined various sweetener real estate business deals offered him in Russia in order to further the Kremlin's cultivation of him.
- However he and his inner circle have accepted a regular flow of intelligence from the Kremlin, including on his Democratic and other political rivals
- Former top Russian intelligence officer claims FSB has compromised TRUMP through his activities in Moscow sufficiently to be able to blackmail him. According to several knowledgeable sources, his conduct in Moscow has included perverted sexual acts which have been arranged/monitored by the FSB
- A dossier of compromising material on Hillary CLINTON has been collated by the Russian Intelligence Services over many years and mainly comprises bugged conversations she had on various visits to Russia and intercepted phone calls rather than any embarrassing conduct. The dossier is controlled by Kremlin spokesman, PESKOV, directly on PUTIN's orders. However it has not as yet been distributed abroad, including to TRUMP. Russian intentions for its deployment still unclear

Detail

1. Speaking to a trusted compatriot in June 2016 sources A and B, a senior Russian Foreign Ministry figure and a former top level Russian intelligence officer still active inside the Kremlin respectively, the Russian authorities had been cultivating and supporting US Republican presidential candidate, Donald TRUMP for at least 5 years. Source B asserted that the TRUMP operation was both supported and directed by Russian President Vladimir PUTIN. Its aim was to sow discord and disunity both within the US itself, but

more especially within the Transatlantic alliance which was viewed as inimical to Russia's interests. Source C, a senior Russian financial official said the TRUMP operation should be seen in terms of PUTIN's desire to return to Nineteenth Century 'Great Power' politics anchored upon countries' interests rather than the ideals-based international order established after World War Two. S/he had overheard PUTIN talking in this way to close associates on several occasions.

2. In terms of specifics, Source A confided that the Kremlin had been feeding TRUMP and his team valuable intelligence on his opponents, including Democratic presidential candidate Hillary CLINTON, for several years (see more below). This was confirmed by Source D, a close associate of TRUMP who had organized and managed his recent trips to Moscow, and who reported, also in June 2016, that this Russian intelligence had been "very helpful". The Kremlin's cultivation operation on TRUMP also had comprised offering him various lucrative real estate development business deals in Russia, especially in relation to the ongoing 2018 World Cup soccer tournament. However, so far, for reasons unknown, TRUMP had not taken up any of these.

3. However, there were other aspects to TRUMP's engagement with the Russian authorities. One which had borne fruit for them was to exploit TRUMP's personal obsessions and sexual perversion in order to obtain suitable 'kompromat' (compromising material) on him. According to Source D, where s/he had been present, TRUMP's (perverted) conduct in Moscow included hiring the presidential suite of the Ritz Carlton Hotel, where he knew President and Mrs OBAMA (whom he hated) had stayed on one of their official trips to Russia, and defiling the bed where they had slept by employing a number of prostitutes to perform a 'golden showers' (urination) show in front of

him. The hotel was known to be under FSB control with microphones and concealed cameras in all the main rooms to record anything they wanted to.

4. The Moscow Ritz Carlton episode involving TRUMP reported above was confirmed by Source E, [REDACTED], who said that s/he and several of the staff were aware of it at the time and subsequently. S/he believed it had happened in

5. Source E provided an introduction for a company ethnic Russian operative to Source F, a female staffer at the hotel when TRUMP had stayed there, who also confirmed the story. Speaking separately in June 2016, Source B (the former top level Russian intelligence officer) asserted that TRUMP's unorthodox behaviour In Russia over the years had provided the authorities there with enough embarrassing material on the now Republican presidential candidate to be able to blackmail him if they so wished.

1. Asked about the Kremlin's reported intelligence feed to TRUMP over recent years and rumours about a Russian dossier of 'kompromat' on Hillary CLINTON (being circulated), Source B confirmed the file's existence. S/he confided in a trusted compatriot that it had been collated by Department K of the FSB for many years, dating back to her husband Bill's presidency, and comprised mainly eavesdropped conversations of various sorts rather than details/evidence of unorthodox or embarrassing behaviour. Some of the conversations were from bugged comments CLINTON had made on her various trips to Russia and focused on things she had said which contradicted her current position on various

issues. Others were most probably from phone intercepts.

2.   Continuing on this theme, Source G, a senior Kremlin official, confided that the CLINTON dossier was controlled exclusively by chief Kremlin spokesman, Dmitriy PESKOV, who was responsible for compiling/handling it on the explicit instructions of PUTIN himself. The dossier however had not as yet been made available abroad, including to TRUMP or his campaign team. At present it was unclear what PUTIN's intentions were in this regard.

20 June 2016
CONFIDENTIAL/SENSITIVE SOURCE

COMPANY INTELLIGENCE REPORT 2016/086

RUSSIA/CYBER CRIME: A SYNOPSIS OF RUSSIAN STATE SPONSORED AND OTHER CYBER OFFENSIVE (CRIMINAL) OPERATIONS

Summary

- Russia has extensive programme of state-sponsored offensive cyber operations. External targets include foreign governments and big corporations, especially banks. FSB leads on cyber within Russian apparatus. Limited success in attacking top foreign targets like G7 governments, security services and IFIs but much more on second tier ones through IT back doors, using corporate and other visitors to Russia
- FSB often uses coercion and blackmail to recruit most capable cyber operatives in Russia into its state-sponsored programmes. Heavy use also, both wittingly and unwittingly,

of CIS émigrés working in western corporations and ethnic Russians employed by neighbouring governments e.g. Latvia

- Example cited of successful Russian cyber operation targeting senior Western business visitor. Provided back door into important Western institutions.
- Example given of US citizen of Russian origin approached by FSB and offered incentive of "investment" in his business when visiting Moscow.
- Problems however for Russian authorities themselves in countering local hackers and cyber criminals, operating outside state control. Central Bank claims there were over 20 serious attacks on correspondent accounts held by CBR in 2015, comprising Roubles several billion in fraud
- Some details given of leading non-state Russian cyber criminal groups

Details

1. Speaking in June 2016, a number of Russian figures with a detailed knowledge of national cyber crime, both state-sponsored and otherwise, outlined the current situation in this area. A former senior intelligence officer divided Russian state-sponsored offensive cyber operations into four categories (in order of priority):- targeting foreign, especially western governments; penetrating leading foreign business corporations, especially banks; domestic monitoring of the elite; and attacking political opponents both at home and abroad. The former intelligence officer reported that the Federal Security Service (FSB~ was the lead organization within the Russian state apparatus for cyber operations.

2. In terms of the success of Russian offensive cyber operations to date, a senior government figure reported that

there had been only limited success in penetrating the "first tier" foreign targets. These comprised western (especially G7 and NATO) governments, security and intelligence services and central banks, and the IFIs. To compensate for this shortfall, massive effort had been invested, with much greater success, in attacking the "secondary targets", particularly western private banks and the governments of smaller states allied to the West. S/he mentioned Latvia in this regard. Hundreds of agents, either consciously cooperating with the FSB or whose personal and professional IT systems had been unwittingly compromised, were recruited. Many were people who had ethnic and family ties to Russia and/or had been incentivized financially to cooperate. Such people often would receive monetary inducements or contractual favours from the Russian state or its agents in return. This had created difficulties for parts of the Russian state apparatus in obliging/indulging them e.g. the Central Bank of Russia knowingly having to cover up for such agents' money laundering operations through the Russian financial system. 3. In terms of the FSB's recruitment of capable cyber operatives to carry out its, ideally deniable, offensive cyber operations, a Russian IT specialist with direct knowledge reported in June 2016 that this was often done using coercion and blackmail. In terms of 'foreign' agents, the FSB was approaching US citizens of Russian Jewish) origin on business trips to Russia. In one case a US citizen of Russian ethnicity had been visiting Moscow to attract investors in his new information technology program. The FSB clearly knew this and had offered to provide seed capital to this person in return for them being able to access and modify his IP, with a view to targeting priority foreign targets by planting a Trojan virus in the software. The US visitor was told this was common practice. The FSB also had implied significant operational success as a result of installing cheap Russian IT games containing their own malware unwittingly by targets on their PCs and other platforms.

4. In a more advanced and successful FSB operation, an IT operator inside a leading Russian SOE, who previously had been employed on conventional (defensive) IT work there, had been under instruction for the last year to conduct an offensive cyber operation against a foreign director of the company. Although the latter was apparently an infrequent visitor to Russia, the FSB now successfully had penetrated his personal IT and through this had managed to access various important institutions in the West through the back door.

5. In terms of other technical IT platforms, an FSB cyber operative flagged up the 'Telegram' enciphered commercial system as having been of especial concern and therefore heavily targeted by the FSB, not least because it was used frequently by Russian internal political activists and oppositionists. His/her understanding was that the FSB now successfully had cracked this communications software and therefore it was no longer secure to use.

6. The senior Russian government figure cited above also reported that non-state sponsored cyber crime was becoming an increasing problem inside Russia for the government and authorities there. The Central Bank of Russia claimed that in 2015 alone there had been more than 20 attempts at serious cyber embezzlement of money from corresponding accounts held there, comprising several billions Roubles. More generally, s/he understood there were circa 15 major organised crime groups in the country involved in cyber crime, all of which continued to operate largely outside state and FSB control. These included the so-called 'Anunak', 'Buktrap' and 'Metel' organisations.

26 July 2015

CONFIDENTIAL/SENSITIVE SOURCE

COMPANY INTELLIGENCE REPORT 2016/095

RUSSIA/US PRESIDENTIAL ELECTION: FURTHER INDICATIONS OF EXTENSIVE CONSPIRACY BETWEEN TRUMP'S CAMPAIGN TEAM AND THE KREMLIN

Summary

- Further evidence of extensive conspiracy between TRUMP's campaign team and Kremlin, sanctioned at highest levels and involving Russian diplomatic staff based in the US
- TRUMP associate admits Kremlin behind recent appearance of DNC emails on WikiLeaks, as means of maintaining plausible deniability
- Agreed exchange of information established in both directions. TRUMP's team using moles within DNC and hackers in the US as well as outside in Russia. PUTIN motivated by fear and hatred of Hillary CLINTON. Russians receiving intel from TRUMP's team on Russian oligarchs and their families in US
- Mechanism for transmitting this intelligence involves "pension" disbursements to Russian emigres living in US as cover, using consular officials in New York, DC and Miami
- Suggestion from source close to TRUMP and MANAFORT that Republican campaign team happy to have Russia as media bogeyman to mask more extensive corrupt business ties to China and other emerging countries

Detail

1. Speaking in confidence to a compatriot in late July 2016, Source E, an ethnic Russian close associate of Republican US presidential candidate Donald TRUMP, admitted that there was a well-developed conspiracy of co-operation between them and the Russian leadership. This was managed on the TRUMP side by the Republican candidate's campaign manager, Paul MANAFORT, who was using foreign policy advisor, Carter PAGE, and others as intermediaries. The two sides had a mutual interest in defeating Democratic presidential candidate Hillary CLINTON, whom President PUTIN apparently both hated and feared.

2. Inter alia, Source E, acknowledged that the Russian regime had been behind the recent leak of embarrassing e-mail messages, emanating from the Democratic National Committee (DNC), to the WikiLeaks platform. The reason for using WikiLeaks was "plausible deniability" and the operation had been conducted with the full knowledge and support of TRUMP and senior members of his campaign team. In return the TRUMP team had agreed to sideline Russian intervention in Ukraine as a campaign issue and to raise US/NATO defence commitments in the Baltics and Eastern Europe to deflect attention away from Ukraine, a priority for PUTIN who needed to cauterise the subject.

3. In the wider context of TRUMP campaign/Kremlin co-operation, Source E claimed that the intelligence network being used against CLINTON comprised three elements. Firstly there were agents/facilitators within the Democratic Party structure itself; secondly Russian émigré and associated offensive cyber operators based in the US; and thirdly, state-sponsored cyber operatives working in Russia. All three elements had played an important role to date. On the mechanism for rewarding relevant assets based in the US, and effecting a two-way flow of intelligence and other useful information, Source E claimed that Russian

diplomatic staff in key cities such as New York, Washington DC and Miami were using the émigré 'pension' distribution system as cover. The operation therefore depended on key people in the US Russian émigré community for its success. Tens of thousands of dollars were involved.

4. In terms of the intelligence flow from the TRUMP team to Russia, Source E reported that much of this concerned the activities of business oligarchs and their families' activities and assets in the US, with which PUTIN and the Kremlin seemed preoccupied.

5. Commenting on the negative media publicity surrounding alleged Russian interference in the US election campaign in support of TRUMP, Source E said he understood that the Republican candidate and his team were relatively relaxed about this because it deflected media and the Democrats' attention away from TRUMP's business dealings in China and other emerging markets. Unlike in Russia, these were substantial and involved the payment of large bribes and kickbacks which, were they to become public, would be potentially very damaging to their campaign.

6. Finally, regarding TRUMP's claimed minimal investment profile in Russia, a separate source with direct knowledge said this had not been for want of trying. TRUMP's previous efforts had included exploring the real estate sector in St Petersburg as well as Moscow but in the end TRUMP had had to settle for the use of extensive sexual services there from local prostitutes rather than business success.

Note: Date page omitted from Buzzfeed copy of this memo.

COMPANY INTELLIGENCE REPORT 2016/94

RUSSIA: SECRET KREMLIN MEETINGS ATTENDED BY TRUMP
ADVISOR, CARTER PAGE IN MOSCOW (JULY 2016)

Summary

- TRUMP advisor Carter PAGE holds secret meetings in
Moscow with SECHIN and senior Kremlin Internal Affairs
official, DIVYEKIN
- SECHIN raises issues of future bilateral US-Russia energy
co-operation and associated lifting of western sanctions
against Russia over Ukraine. PAGE non-committal in
response
- DIVEYKIN discusses release of Russian dossier of
'kompromat' on TRUMP's opponent, Hillary CLINTON, but
also hints at Kremlin possession of such material on TRUMP

Detail

1. Speaking in July 2016, a Russian source close to Rosneft
President, PUTIN close associate and US-sanctioned
individual, Igor SECHIN, confided the details of a recent
secret meeting between him and visiting Foreign Affairs
Advisor to Republican presidential candidate Donald
TRUMP, Carter PAGE.
2. According to SECHIN's associate, the Rosneft President
(CEO) had raised with PAGE the issues of future bilateral
energy cooperation and prospects for an associated move to
lift Ukraine-related western sanctions against Russia. PAGE
had reacted positively to this demarche by SECHIN but had
been generally non-committal in response.

3. Speaking separately, also in July 2016, an official close to Presidential Administration Head, S. IVANOV, confided in a compatriot that a senior colleague in the Internal Political Department of the PA, DIVYEKIN (nfd) also had met secretly with PAGE on his recent visit. Their agenda had included DIVEYKIN raising a dossier of 'kompromat' the Kremlin possessed on TRUMP's Democratic presidential rival, Hillary CLINTON, and its possible release to the Republican's campaign team.

4. However, the Kremlin official close to S. IVANOV added that s/he believed DIVEYKIN also had hinted [or indicated more strongly} that the Russian leadership also had 'kompromat' on TRUMP which the latter should bear in mind in his dealings with them.

19 July 2016

COMPANY INTELLIGENCE REPORT 2016/097

RUSSIA-US PRESIDENTIAL ELECTION: KREMLIN CONCERN THAT POLITICAL FALLOUT FROM DNC E-MAIL HACKING AFFAIR SPIRALLING OUT OF CONTROL

Summary

• Kremlin concerned that political fallout from DNC e-mail hacking operation is spiralling out of control. Extreme nervousness among TRUMP's associates as result of negative media attention/accusations

- Russians meanwhile keen to cool situation and maintain 'plausible deniability' of existing/ongoing pro-TRUMP and anti-CLINTON operations. Therefore unlikely to be any ratcheting up offensive plays in immediate future
- Source close to TRUMP campaign however confirms regular exchange with Kremlin has existed for at least 8 years, including intelligence fed back to Russia on oligarchs' activities in US
- Russians apparently have promised not to use 'kompromat' they hold on TRUMP as leverage, given high levels of voluntary co-operation forthcoming from his team

Detail

1. Speaking in confidence to a trusted associate in late July 2016, a Russian émigré figure close to the Republican US presidential candidate Donald TRUMP's campaign team commented on the fallout from publicity surrounding the Democratic National Committee (DNC) e-mail hacking scandal. The émigré said there was a high level of anxiety within the TRUMP team as a result of various accusations levelled against them and indications from the Kremlin that President PUTIN and others in the leadership thought things had gone too far now and risked spiralling out of control.
2. Continuing on this theme, the émigré associate of TRUMP opined that the Kremlin wanted the situation to calm but for 'plausible deniability' to be maintained concerning its (extensive) pro-TRUMP and anti-CLINTON operations. S/he therefore judged that it was unlikely these would be ratcheted up, at least for the time being.
3. However, in terms of established operational liaison between the TRUMP team and the Kremlin, the émigré confirmed that an intelligence exchange had been running

between them for at least 8 years. Within this context PUTIN's priority requirement had been for intelligence on the activities, business and otherwise, in the US of leading Russian oligarchs and their families. TRUMP and his associates duly had obtained and supplied the Kremlin with this information.

4. Finally, the émigré said s/he understood the Kremlin had more intelligence on CLINTON and her campaign but he did not know the details or when or if it would be released. As far as 'kompromat' (compromising information) on TRUMP were concerned, although there was plenty of this, he understood the Kremlin had given its word that it would not be deployed against the Republican presidential candidate given how helpful and co-operative his team had been over several years, and particularly of late.

30 July 2016

COMPANY INTELLIGENCE REPORT 2016/100

RUSSIA/USA: GROWING BACKLASH IN KREMLIN TO DNC HACKING AND TRUMP SUPPORT OPERATIONS

Summary

- Head of PA IVANOV laments Russian intervention in US presidential election and black PR against CLINTON and the

DNC. Vows not to supply intelligence to Kremlin PR operatives again. Advocates now sitting tight and denying everything

- Presidential spokesman PESKOV the main protagonist in Kremlin campaign to aid TRUMP and damage CLINTON. He is now scared and fears being made scapegoat by leadership for backlash in US. Problem compounded by his botched intervention in recent Turkish crisis

- Premier MEDVEDEV's office furious over DNC hacking and associated anti-Russian publicity. Want good relations with US and ability to travel there. Refusing to support or help cover up after PESKOV

- Talk now in Kremlin of TRUMP withdrawing from presidential race altogether, but this still largely wishful thinking by more liberal elements in Moscow

Detail

1. Speaking in early August 2016, two well-placed and established Kremlin sources outlined the divisions and backlash in Moscow arising from the leaking of Democratic National Committee (DNC) e-mails and the wider pro-TRUMP operation being conducted in the US. Head of Presidential Administration, Sergei IVANOV, was angry at the recent turn of events. He believed the Kremlin "team" involved, led by presidential spokesman Dmitriy PESKOV, had gone too far in interfering in foreign affairs with their "elephant in a china shop black PW'. IVANOV claimed always to have opposed the handling and exploitation of intelligence by this PR "team". Following the backlash against such foreign interference in US politics, IVANOV was advocating that the only sensible course of action now for

the Russian leadership was to "sit tight and deny everything".

2. Continuing on this theme the source close to IVANOV reported that PESKOV now was "scared shitless" that he would be scapegoated by PUTIN and the Kremlin and held responsible for the backlash against Russian political interference in the US election. IVANOV was determined to stop PESKOV playing an independent role in relation to the US going forward and the source fully expected the presidential spokesman now to lay low. PESKOV's position was not helped by a botched attempt by him also to interfere in the recent failed coup in Turkey from a government relations (GR) perspective (no further details).

3. The extent of disquiet and division within Moscow caused by the backlash against Russian interference in the US election was underlined by a second source, close to premier Dmitriy MEDVEDEV (DAM). S/he said the Russian prime minister and his colleagues wanted to have good relations with the US, regardless of who was in power there, and not least so as to be able to travel there in future, either officially or privately. They were openly refusing to cover up for PESKOV and others involved in the DNC/TRUMP operations or to support his counter-attack of allegations against the USG for its alleged hacking of the Russian government and state agencies.

4. According to the first source, close to IVANOV, there had been talk in the Kremlin of TRUMP being forced to withdraw from the presidential race altogether as a result of recent events, ostensibly on grounds of his psychological state and unsuitability for high office. This might not be so bad for Russia in the circumstances but in the view of the source, it remained largely wishful thinking on the part of those in the regime opposed to PESKOV and his "botched" operations, at least for the time being.

5 August 2016

COMPANY INTELLIGENCE REPORT 2016/101

RUSSIA/US PRESIDENTIAL ELECTION: SENIOR KREMLIN FIGURE OUTLINES EVOLVING RUSSIAN TACTICS IN PRO-TRUMP, ANTI-CLINTON OPERATION

Summary

- Head of PA, IVANOV assesses Kremlin intervention in US presidential election and outlines leadership thinking on operational way forward
- No new leaks envisaged, as too politically risky, but rather further exploitation of (WikiLeaks) material already disseminated to exacerbate divisions
- Educated US youth to be targeted as protest (against CLINTON) and swing vote in attempt to turn them over to TRUMP
- Russian leadership, including PUTIN, celebrating perceived success to date in splitting US hawks and elite
- Kremlin engaging with several high profile US players, including STEIN, PAGE and (former DIA Director Michael Flynn), and funding their recent visits to Moscow

Details

1. Speaking in confidence to a close colleague in early August 2016, Head of the Russian Presidential Administration (PA), Sergei IVANOV, assessed the impact and results of Kremlin intervention in the US presidential

election to date. Although most commentators believed that the Kremlin was behind the leaked DNC/CLINTON e-mails, this remained technically deniable. Therefore the Russians would not risk their position for the time being with new leaked material, even to a third party like WikiLeaks. Rather the tactics would be to spread rumours and misinformation about the content of what al ready had been leaked and make up new content.

2. Continuing on this theme, IVANOV said that the audience to be targeted by such operations was the educated youth in America as the PA assessed that there was still a chance they could be persuaded to vote for Republican candidate Donald TRUMP as a protest against the Washington establishment (in the form of Democratic candidate Hillary CLINNTON). The hope was that even if she won, as a result of this CLINTON in power would be bogged down in working for internal reconciliation in the US, rather than being able to focus on foreign policy which would damage Russia's interests. This also should give President PUTIN more room for manoeuvre in the run-up to Russia's own presidential election in 2018.

3. IVANOV reported that although the Kremlin had underestimated the strength of US media and liberal reaction to the DNC hack and TRUMP's links to Russia, PUTIN was generally satisfied with the progress of the anti-CLINTON operation to date. He recently had had a drink with PUTIN to mark this. In IVANOV's view, the US had tried to divide the Russian elite with sanctions but failed, whilst they, by contrast, had succeeded in splitting the US hawks inimical to Russia and the Washington elite more generally, half of whom had refused to endorse any presidential candidate as a result of Russian intervention.

4. Speaking separately, also in early August 2016, a Kremlin official involved in US relations commented on aspects of

the Russian operation to date. Its goals had been threefold -
asking sympathetic US actors how Moscow could help them;
gathering relevant intelligence; and creating and
disseminating compromising information ('kompromat').
This had involved the Kremlin supporting various US
political figures, including funding indirectly their recent
visits to Moscow. S/he named a delegation from Lyndon
LAROUCHE; presidential candidate Jill STEIN of the Green
Party; TRUMP foreign policy adviser Carter PAGE; and
former DIA Director Michael Flynn, in this regard and as
successful in terms of perceived outcomes.

10 August 2016

COMPANY INTELLIGENCE REPORT 2016/102

RUSSIA/US PRESIDENTIAL ELECTION: REACTION IN TRUMP CAMP
TO RECENT NEGATIVE PUBLICITY ABOUT RUSSIAN INTERFERENCE
AND LIKELY RESULTING TACTICS GOING FORWARD

Summary

- TRUMP campaign insider reports recent DNC e-mail leaks
were aimed at switching SANDERS (protest) voters away
from CLINTON and over to TRUMP
- Admits Republican campaign underestimated resulting
negative reaction from US liberals, elite and media and
forced to change course as result
- Need now to turn tables on CLINTON's use of PUTIN as
bogeyman in election, although some resentment at Russian

president's perceived attempt to undermine USG and system over and above swinging presidential election

Detail

1. Speaking in confidence on 9 August 2016, an ethnic Russian associate of Republican US presidential candidate Donald TRUMP discussed the reaction inside his camp, and revised tactics therein resulting from recent negative publicity concerning Moscow's clandestine involvement in the campaign. TRUMP's associate reported that the aim of leaking the DNC e-mails to WikiLeaks during the Democratic Convention had been to swing supporters of Bernie SANDERS away from Hillary CLINTON and across to TRUMP. These voters were perceived as activist and anti-status quo and anti-establishment and in that regard sharing many features with the TRUMP campaign, including a visceral dislike of Hillary CLINTON. This objective had been conceived and promoted, inter alia, by TRUMP's foreign policy adviser Carter PAGE who had discussed it directly with the ethnic Russian associate.

2. Continuing on this theme, the ethnic Russian associate of TRUMP assessed that the problem was that the TRUMP campaign had underestimated the strength of the negative reaction from liberals and especially the conservative elite to Russian interference. This was forcing a rethink and a likely change of tactics. The main objective in the short term was to check Democratic candidate Hillary CLINTON's successful exploitation of the PUTIN as bogeyman/Russian interference story to tarnish TRUMP and bolster her own (patriotic) credentials. The TRUMP campaign was focusing on tapping into support in the American television media to

achieve this, as they reckoned this resource had been underused by them to date.

3. However, TRUMP's associate also admitted that there was a fair amount of anger and resentment within the Republican candidate's team at what was perceived by PUTIN as going beyond the objective of weakening CLINTON and bolstering TRUMP, by attempting to exploit the situation to undermine the US government and democratic system more generally. It was unclear at present how this aspect of the situation would play out in the weeks to come.

10 August 2016

COMPANY INTELLIGENCE REPORT 2016/136
#RUSSIA/US PRESIDENTIAL ELECTION: FURTHER DETAILS OF TRUMP LAWYER COHEN'S SECRET LIAISON WITH THE KREMLIN

Summary

- Kremlin insider reports TRUMP lawyer COHEN's secret meeting/s with Kremlin officials in August 2016 was/were held in Prague
- Russian parastatal organisation Rossotrudnichestvo used as cover for this liaison and premises in Czech capital may have been used for the meeting/s
- Pro-PUTIN leading Duma figure, KOSACHEV, reportedly involved as "plausibly deniable" facilitator and may have participated in the August meeting/s with COHEN

Detail

1. Speaking to a compatriot and friend on 19 October 2016, a Kremlin insider provided further details of reported clandestine meeting/s between Republican presidential

candidate, Donald TRUMP's lawyer Michael COHEN and Kremlin representatives in August 2016. Although the communication between them had to be cryptic for security reasons, the Kremlin insider clearly indicated to his/her friend that the reported contact/s took place in Prague, Czech Republic.

2. Continuing on this theme, the Kremlin insider highlighted the importance of the Russian parastatal organisation, Rossotrudnichestvo, in this contact between TRUMP campaign representative/s and Kremlin officials. Rossotrudnichestvo was being used as cover for this relationship and its office in Prague may well have been used to host the COHEN/Russian Presidential Administration (PA) meeting/s. It was considered a "plausibly deniable" vehicle for this, whilst remaining entirely under Kremlin control.

3. The Kremlin insider went on to identify leading pro-PUTIN Duma figure, Konstantin KOSACHEV (Head of the Foreign Relations Committee) as an important figure in the TRUMP campaign-Kremlin liaison operation. KOSACHEV, also "plausibly deniable" being part of the Russian legislature rather than executive, had facilitated the contact in Prague and by implication, may have attended the meeting / s with COHEN there in August.

Company Comment

We reported previously, in our Company Intelligence Report 2016/135 of 19 October 2016 from the same source, that COHEN met officials from the PA Legal Department clandestinely in an EU country in August 2016. This was in order to clean up the mess left behind by western media revelations of TRUMP ex-campaign manager MANAFORT's corrupt relationship with the former pro-Russian

YANUKOVYCH regime in Ukraine and TRUMP foreign policy advisor, Carter PAGE's secret meetings in Moscow with senior regime figures in July 2016. According to the Kremlin advisor, these meeting/s were originally scheduled for COHEN in Moscow but shifted to what was considered an operationally "soft" EU country when it was judged too compromising for him to travel to the Russian capital.

20 October 2016

COMPANY INTELLIGENCE REPORT 2016/105

RUSSIA/UKRAINE: THE DEMISE OF TRUMP'S CAMPAIGN MANAGER PAUL MANAFORT

Summary

- Ex-Ukrainian President YANUKOVYCH confides directly to PUTIN that he authorised kick-back payments to MANAFORT, as alleged in western media. Assures Russian President however there is no documentary evidence/trail
- PUTIN and Russian leadership remain worried however and sceptical that YANUKOVYCH has fully covered the traces of these payments to TRUMP's former campaign manager
- Close associate of TRUMP explains reasoning behind MANAFORT's recent resignation. Ukraine revelations played part but others wanted MANAFORT out for various reasons, especially LEWANDOWSKI who remains influential

Detail

1. Speaking in late August 2016, in the immediate aftermath of Paul MANAFORT's resignation as campaign manager for US Republican presidential candidate Donald TRUMP, a well-placed Russian figure reported on a recent meeting between President PUTIN and ex-President YANUKOVYCH of Ukraine. This had been held in secret on 15 August near Volgograd, Russia and the western media revelations about MANAFORT and Ukraine had featured prominently on the agenda. YANUKOVYCH had confided in PUTIN that he did authorise and order substantial kick-back payments to MANAFORT as alleged but sought to reassure him that there was no documentary trail left behind which could provide clear evidence of this.

2. Given YANUKOVYCH's (unimpressive) record in covering up his own corrupt tracks in the past, PUTIN and others in the Russian leadership were sceptical about the ex-Ukrainian president's reassurances on this as relating to MANAFORT. They therefore still feared the scandal had legs, especially as MANAFORT had been commercially active in Ukraine right up to the time (in March 2016) when he joined TRUMP's campaign team. For them it therefore remained a point of potential political vulnerability and embarrassment.

3. Speaking separately, also in late August 2016, an American political figure associated with Donald TRUMP and his campaign outlined the reasons behind MANAFORT's recent demise. S/he said it was true that the Ukraine corruption revelations had played a part in this but also, several senior players close to TRUMP had wanted MANAFORT out, primarily to loosen his control on strategy and policy formulation. Of particular importance in this regard was MANAFORT's predecessor as campaign manager, Corey LEWANDOWSKI, who hated MANAFORT personally and remained close to TRUMP with whom he discussed the presidential campaign on a regular basis.

22 August 2016

COMPANY INTELLIGENCE REPORT 2016/111

RUSSIA/US: KREMLIN FALLOUT FROM MEDIA EXPOSURE OF MOSCOW'S INTERFERENCE IN THE US PRESIDENTIAL CAMPAIGN

Summary

- Kremlin orders senior staff to remain silent in media and private on allegations of Russian interference in US presidential campaign
- Senior figure however confirms gist of allegations and reports IVANOV sacked as Head of Administration on account of giving PUTIN poor advice on issue. VAINO selected as his replacement partly because he was not involved in pro-TRUMP, anti-CLINTON operation/s
- Russians do have further 'kompromat' on CLINTON (e-mails) and considering disseminating it after Duma (legislative elections) in late September. Presidential spokesman PESKOV continues to lead on this
- However, equally important is Kremlin objective to shift policy consensus favourably to Russia in US post-OBAMA whoever wins. Both presidential candidates' opposition to TPP and TTIP viewed as a result in this respect
- Senior Russian diplomat withdrawn from Washington embassy on account of potential exposure in US presidential election operation/s

Detail

1. Speaking in confidence to a trusted compatriot in mid-September 2016, a senior member of the Russian Presidential Administration (PA) commented on the political fallout from recent western media revelations about Moscow's intervention, in favour of Donald TRUMP and against Hillary CLINTON, in the US presidential election. The PA official reported that the issue had become incredibly sensitive and that President PUTIN had issued direct orders that Kremlin and government insiders should not discuss it in public or even in private.

2. Despite this, the PA official confirmed, from direct knowledge, that the gist of the allegations was true. PUTIN had been receiving conflicting advice on interfering from three separate and expert groups. On one side had been the Russian ambassador to the US, Sergei KISLYAK, and the Ministry of Foreign Affairs, together with an independent and informal network run by presidential foreign policy advisor, Yuri USHAKOV (KISLYAK's predecessor in Washington) who had urged caution and the potential negative impact on Russia from the operation/s. On the other side was former PA Head, Sergei IVANOV, backed by Russian Foreign Intelligence (SVR), who had advised PUTIN that the pro-TRUMP, anti CLINTON operation/s would be both effective and plausibly deniable with little blowback. The first group/s had been proven right and this had been the catalyst in PUTIN's decision to sack IVANOV (unexpectedly) as PA Head in August. His successor, Anton VAINO, had been selected for the job partly because he had not been involved in the US presidential election operation/s.

3. Continuing on this theme, the senior PA official said the situation now was that the Kremlin had further 'kompromat' on candidate CLINTON and had been considering releasing this via "plausibly deniable" channels after the Duma

(legislative) elections were out of the way in mid September, There was however a growing train of thought and associated lobby, arguing that the Russians could still make candidate CLINTON look "weak and stupid" by provoking her into railing against PUTIN and Russia without the need to release more of her e-mails. Presidential Spokesman, Dmitriy PESKOV remained a key figure in the operation, although any final decision on dissemination of further material would be taken by PUTIN himself.

4. The senior PA official also reported that a growing element in Moscow's intervention in the US presidential election campaign was the objective of shifting the US political consensus in Russia's perceived interests regardless of who won. It basically comprised of pushing candidate CLINTON away from President OBAMA's policies. The best example of this was that both candidates now openly opposed the draft trade agreements, TPP and TTIP, which were assessed by Moscow as detrimental to Russian interests. Other issues where the Kremlin was looking to shift the US policy consensus were Ukraine and Syria. Overall however, the presidential election was considered still to he too close to call.

5. Finally, speaking separately to the same compatriot, a senior Russian MFA official reported that as a prophylactic measure, a leading Russian diplomat, Mikhail KULAGIN, had been withdrawn from Washington at short notice because Moscow feared his heavy involvement in the US presidential election operation, including the so-called veterans' pensions ruse (reported previously), would be exposed in the media there. His replacement, Andrei BONDAREV however was clean in this regard.

Company Comment

The substance of what was reported by the senior Russian PA official in paras 1 and 2 above, including the reasons for Sergei IVANOV's dismissal, was corroborated independently by a former top level Russian intelligence officer and Kremlin insider, also in mid-September.

14 September 2016

COMPANY INTELLIGENCE REPORT 2016/112

RUSSIA/US PRESIDENTIAL ELECTION: KREMLIN-ALPHA GROUP COOPERATION

Summary

- Top level Russian official confirms current closeness of Alpha Group PUTIN relationship. Significant favours continue to be done in both directions and FRIDMAN and AVEN still giving informal advice to PUTIN, especially on the US
- Key intermediary in PUTIN-Alpha relationship identified as Oleg GOVORUN, currently Head of a Presidential Administration department but throughout the 1990s, the Alpha executive who delivered illicit cash directly to PUTIN
- PUTIN personally unbothered about Alpha's current lack of investment in Russia but under pressure from colleagues over this and able to exploit it as lever over Alpha interlocutors

Detail

1. Speaking to a trusted compatriot in mid-September 2016, a top level Russian government official commented on the history and current state of relations between President PUTIN and the Alpha Group of businesses led by oligarchs Mikhail FRIDMAN, Petr AVEN and German KHAN. The Russian government figure reported that although they had had their ups and downs, the leading figures in Alpha currently were on very good terms with PUTIN. Significant favours continued to be done in both directions, primarily political ones for PUTIN and business/legal ones for Alpha. Also, FRIDMAN and AVEN continued to give informal advice to PUTIN on foreign policy, and especially about the US where he distrusted advice being given to him by officials.

2. Although FRIDMAN recently had met directly with PUTIN in Russia, much of the dialogue and business between them was mediated through a senior Presidential Administration official, Oleg GOVORUN, who currently headed the department therein responsible for Social Co-operation With the CIS. GOVORUN was trusted by PUTIN and recently had accompanied him to Uzbekistan to pay respects at the tomb of former president KARIMOV. However according to the top level Russian government official, during the 1990s GOVORUN had been Head of Government Relations at Alpha Group and in reality, the "driver" and "bag carrier" used by FRIDMAN and AVEN to deliver large amounts of illicit cash to the Russian president, at that time deputy Mayor of St Petersburg. Given that and the continuing sensitivity of the PUTIN-Alpha relationship, and need for plausible deniability, much of the contact between them was now indirect and entrusted to the relatively low profile GOVORUN.

3. The top level Russian government official described the PUTIN-Alpha relationship as both carrot and stick. Alpha held 'kompromat' on PUTIN and his corrupt business

activities from the 1990s whilst although not personally overly bothered by Alpha's failure to reinvest the proceeds of its TNK oil company sale into the Russian economy since, the Russian president was able to use pressure on this count from senior Kremlin colleagues as a lever on FRIDMAN and AVEN to make them do his political bidding.

14 September 2016

COMPANY INTELLIGENCE REPORT 2016/113

RUSSIA/US PRESIDENTIAL ELECTION- REPUBLICAN CANDIDATE TRUMP'S PRIOR ACTIVITIES IN ST PETERSBURG

Summary

- Two knowledgeable St Petersburg sources claim Republican candidate TRUMP has paid bribes and engaged in sexual activities there but key witnesses silenced and evidence hard to obtain
- Both believe Azeri business associate of TRUMP, Araz AGALAROV will know the details

Detail

1. Speaking to a trusted compatriot in September 2016, two well-placed sources based in St Petersburg, one in the political/business elite and the other involved in the local services and tourist industry, commented on Republican US presidential candidate Donald TRUMP's prior activities in the city.

2. Both knew TRUMP had visited St Petersburg on several occasions in the past and had been interested in doing business deals there involving real estate. The local business/political elite figure reported that TRUMP had paid bribes there to further his interests but very discreetly and only through affiliated companies, making it very hard to prove. The local services industry source reported that TRUMP had participated in sex parties in the city too, but that all direct witnesses to this recently had been "silenced" i.e. bribed or coerced to disappear.

3. The two St Petersburg figures cited believed an Azeri business figure, Araz AGAKAROV (with offices in Baku and London) had been closely involved with TRUMP in Russia and would know most of the details of what the Republican presidential candidate had got up to there.

14 September 2016

COMPANY INTELLIGENCE REPORT 2018/130

RUSSIA: KREMLIN ASSESSMENT OF TRUMP AND RUSSIAN INTERFERENCE IN US PRESIDENTIAL ELECTION

Summary

- Buyer's remorse sets in with Kremlin over TRUMP support operation In US presidential election. Russian leadership disappointed that leaked emails on CLINTON have not had greater Impact in campaign
- Russians have Injected further anti-CLINTON material Into the 'plausibly deniable' leeks pipeline which will €continue to surface, but best material already In public domain

- PUTIN angry with senior officials who "overpromised" on TRUMP and further heads likely to roll as result. Foreign Mlnister LAVROV may be next
- TRUMP supported by Kremlin because seen as divisive, anti-establishment candldate who would shake up current international status quo in Russia's favour. Lead on TRUMP operation moved from Foreign Ministry to FSB and then to presidential administration where It now sits

Detail

1. Speaking separately in confidence to a trusted compatriot In early October 2016, a senior Russian leadership figure and a Foreign Ministry official reported on recent developments concerning the Kremlin's operation to support Republican candidate Donald TRUMP in the US presidential election. The senior leadership figure said that a degree of buyer's remorse was setting in among Russian leaders concerning TRUMP. PUTIN and his colleagues were surprised and disappointed that leaks of Democratic candidate Hillary CLINTON's hacked emails had not had greater impact on the campaign.

2. Continuing on this theme, the senior leadership figure commented that a stream of further hacked CLINTON material already had been injected by the Kremlin into compliant western media outlets like WikiLeaks, which remained al least "plausibly deniable", so the stream of these would continue through October and up to the election. However s/he understood the best material the Russians had already was out and there were no real game-changers to come.

3. The Russian Foreign Ministry official, who had direct access to the TRUMP support operation, reported that

PUTIN was angry at his subordinate's "over-promising" on the Republican presidential candidate, both in terms of his chances and reliability and being able to cover and/or contain the US backlash over Kremlin interference. More heads therefore were likely to roll, with the MFA the easiest target. Ironically, despite his consistent urging of caution on the issue, Foreign Minister LAVROV could be the next one to go.

4. Asked to explain why PUTIN and the Kremlin had launched such an aggressive TRUMP support operation in the first place, the MFA official said that Russia needed to upset the liberal international status quo, including on Ukraine-related sanctions, which was seriously disadvantaging the country. TRUMP was viewed as divisive in disrupting the whole US political system: anti-Establishment; and a pragmatist with whom they could do business. As the TRUMP support operation had gained momentum, €control of It had passed Item the MFA to the FSB and then into the presidential administration where it remained, a reflection of Its growing significance over time. There was still a view in the Kremlin that TRUMP would continue as a (divisive) political force even if he lost the presidency and may run for and be elected to another public office.

12 October 2016

COMPANY INTELLIGENCE REPORT 2016/134

RUSSIA/US PRESIDENTIAL ELECTION: FURTHER DETAILS OF KREMLIN LIAISON WITH TRUMP CAMPAIGN

Summary

- Close associate of SECHIN confirms his secret meeting in Moscow with Carter PAGE in July
- Substance included offer of large stake in Rosneft in return for lifting sanctions on Russia. PAGE confirms this is TRUMP's intention
- SECHIN continued to think TRUMP could win presidency up to 17 October. Now looking to reorientate his engagement with the US
- Kremlin insider highlights importance of TRUMP's lawyer, Michael COHEN in covert relationship with Russia. COHEN's wife is of Russian descent and her father a leading property developer in Moscow

Detail

1. Speaking to a trusted compatriot in mid October 2016, a dose associate of Rosneft President and PUTIN ally Igor' SECHIN elaborated on the reported secret meeting between the latter and Carter PAGE, of US Republican presidential candidate's foreign policy team, in Moscow in July 2016. The secret meeting had been confirmed to him/her by a senior member of SECHIN's staff, in addition to by the Rosneft President himself. It took place on either 7 or 8 July, the same day or the one after Carter PAGE to the Higher Economic School in Moscow.

2. In terms of the substance of their discussion, SECHIN's associate said that the Rosneft President was so keen to lift personal and corporate western sanctions imposed on the company~ that he offered PAGE/TRUMP's associates the brokerage of up to a 19 per cent (privatised) stake in Rosneft in return. PAGE had expressed interest and confirmed that were TRUMP elected US president, then sanctions on Russia would be lifted.

3. According to SECHIN's dose associate, the Rosneft President had continued to believe that TRUMP could win the US presidency right up to 17 October, when he assessed this was no longer possible. SECHIN was keen to re-adapt accordingly and put feelers out to other business and political contacts in the US instead.

4. Speaking separately to the same compatriot in mid-October 2016, a Kremlin insider with direct access to the leadership confirmed that a key role in the secret TRUMP campaign/Kremlin relationship was being played by the Republican candidate's personal lawyer Michael COHEN. [REDACTED].

Source Comment

1. SECHIN's associate opined that although PAGE had not stated it explicitly to SECHIN, he had clearly implied that in terms of his comment on TRUMP's intention to lift Russian sanctions if elected president, he was speaking with the Republican candidate's authority.

Company Comment

1. [REDACTED].
18 October 2016

COMPANY INTELLIGENCE REPORT 2016/135

RUSSIA/US PRESIDENTIAL ELECTION: THE IMPORTANT ROLE OF TRUMP LAWYER, COHEN IN CAMPAIGN'S SECRET LIAISON WITH THE KREMLIN

Summary

- Kremlin insider outlines important role played by TRUMP's lawyer COHEN in secret liaison with Russian leadership
- COHEN engaged with Russians in trying to cover up scandal of MANAFORT and exposure of PAGE and meets Kremlin officials secretly in the EU in August in pursuit of this goal
- These secret contacts continue but are now farmed out to trusted agents in Kremlin-linked institutes so as to remain "plausibly deniable" for Russian regime
- Further confirmation that sacking of IVANOV and appointments of VAINO and KIRIYENKO linked to need to cover up Kremlin's TRUMP support operation

Detail

1. Speaking in confidence to a longstanding compatriot friend in mid October 2016, a Kremlin insider highlighted the importance of Republican presidential candidate Donald TRUMP's lawyer, Michael COHEN, in the ongoing secret liaison relationship between the New York tycoon's campaign and the Russian leadership. COHEN's role had grown following the departure of Paul MANAFORT as TRUMP's campaign manager in August 2016. Prior to that MANAFORT had led for the TRUMP side.

2. According to the Kremlin insider, COHEN now was heavily engaged in a cover up and damage limitation operation in the attempt to prevent the full details of TRUMP's relationship with Russia being exposed. In pursuit of this aim, COHEN had met secretly with several Russian Presidential Administration (PA) Legal Department officials

in an EU country in August 2016. The immediate issues had been to contain further scandals involving MANAFORT's commercial and political role in Russia/Ukraine and to limit the damage arising from exposure of former TRUMP foreign policy advisor, Carter PAGE's secret meetings with Russian leadership figures in Moscow the previous month. The overall objective had been to "to sweep it all under the carpet and make sure no connections could be fully established or proven"

3. Things had become even "hotter" since August on the TRUMP-Russia track. According to the Kremlin insider, this had meant that direct contact between the TRUMP team and Russia had been farmed out by the Kremlin to trusted agents of influence working in pro-government policy institutes like that of Law and Comparative Jurisprudence. COHEN however continued to lead for the TRUMP team.

4. Referring back to the (surprise) sacking of Sergei IVANOV as Head of PA in August 2016, his replacement by Anton VAINO and the appointment of former Russian premier Sergei KIRIYENKO to another senior position in the PA, the Kremlin insider repeated that this had been directly connected to the TRUMP support operation and the need to cover up now that it was being exposed by the USG and in the western media.

Company Comment

The Kremlin insider was unsure of the identities of the PA officials with whom COHEN met secretly in August, or the exact date/s and locations of the meeting/s. There were significant internal security barriers being erected in the PA as the TRUMP issue became more controversial and damaging. However s/he continued to try to obtain these.

19 October 2016

COMPANY INTELLIGENCE REPORT 2016/166

US/RUSSIA: FURTHER DETAILS OF SECRET DIALOGUE BETWEEN TRUMP CAMPAIGN TEAM, KREMLIN AND ASSOCIATED HACKERS IN PRAGUE

Summary

- TRUMP's representative COHEN accompanied to Prague in August/September 2016 by 3 colleagues for secret discussions with Kremlin representatives and associated operators/hackers
- Agenda included how to process deniable cash payments to operatives; contingency plans for covering up operations; and action in event of a CLINTON election victory
- Some further details of Russian representatives~operatives involved; Romanian hackers employed; and use of Bulgaria as bolt hole to "lie low"
- Anti-CLINTON hackers and other operatives paid by both TRUMP team and Kremlin, but with ultimate loyalty to Head of PA, IVANOV and his Successor/s

Detail

- We reported previously (2016/135 and/136) on secret meeting/s held in Prague, Czech Republic in August 2016 between then Republican presidential candidate Donald TRUMP's representative, Michael COHEN and his interlocutors from the Kremlin working under cover of Russian 'NGO' Rossotrudnichestvo.

1. [REDACTED] provided further details of these meeting/s and associated anti CLINTON/Democratic Party operations. COHEN had been accompanied to Prague by 3 colleagues and the timing of the visit was either in the last week of August or the first week of September. One of their main Russian interlocutors was Oleg SOLODUKHIN operating under Rossotrudnichestvo cover. According to [REDACTED], the agenda comprised questions on how deniable cash payments were to be made to hackers who had worked in Europe under Kremlin direction against the CLINTON campaign and various contingencies for covering up these operations and Moscow's secret liaison with the TRUMP team more generally.

2. [REDACTED] reported that over the period March-September 2016 a company called XBT/Webziila and its affiliates had been using botnets and porn traffic to transmit viruses, plant bugs, steal data and conduct "altering operations" against the Democratic Party leadership. Entities linked to one [REDACTED] were involved and he and another hacking expert, both recruited under duress by the FSB, Seva KAPSUGOVICH, were significant players in this operation. In Prague, COHEN agreed contingency plans for various scenarios to protect the operation, but in particular what was to be clone in the event that Hillary CLINTON won the presidency, it was important in this event that all cash payments owed were made quickly and discreetly and that cyber and other operators were stood down/able to go effectively to ground to cover their traces. (We reported earlier that the involvement of political operatives Paul MANAFORT and Carter PAGE in the secret TRUMP-Kremlin liaison had been exposed in the media in the run-up to Prague and that damage limitation of these also was discussed by COHEN with the Kremlin representatives}.

3. In terms of practical measures to be taken, it was agreed by the two sides in Prague to stand down various "Romanian hackers" (presumably based in their homeland or neighbouring eastern Europe) and that other operatives should head for a bolt-hole in Plovdiv, Bulgaria where they should "lay low". On payments, IVANOV's associate said that the operatives involved had been paid by both TRUMP's team and the Kremlin, though their orders and ultimate loyalty lay with IVANOV, as Head of the PA and thus ultimately responsible for the operation, and his designated successor/s after he was dismissed by president PUTIN in connection with the anti-CLINTON operation in mid August.

13 December 2016

© mathew 2017

Acknowledgements

It was Lord John Kerr's call to 'Halt Brexit Now' that inspired me to update the previous version of this book which had been sent electronically to a number of my political and other contacts during the campaign for the 8 June General election. I then realised that it may well take some months before there is widespread resentment at Brexit. So in the interim all of us 'remainers' should surely do all we can to make known to as wide an audience as possible why Brexit must be halted and how we can move on to do that.

My thanks also go to Lord 'Paddy' Ashdown whose article in the March 2017 edition of 'Prospect' urging a new political alignment in UK politics inspired me to write this book in the first place. And of course my thanks must go to contacts among the electorate, politicians of all parties, business, banking, media, research scientists and others who have provided the information I have used, for – as I said at the outset – there is here nothing here that has not already been published.

I was particularly encouraged, when preparing this revision, by the positions on Brexit taken by Guy Verhofstadt leader in the European Parliament, Jean-Claude Juncker President of the European Commission, and Michel Barnier European Chief Negotiator for Brexit.

And of course I was greatly helped by those who provided the articles and speeches supporting my own contribution – notably His Holiness Pope Francis, Russia's President Putin, Russian Foreign Minister Sergei Lavrov, Senator Hillary Clinton, Senator Robert Byrd, Labour Party Leader Jeremy Corbyn, Roger Cohen and Paul Krugman of The New York Times, Mary Dejevsky of The Guardian, Kim Sengupta of The Independent and not least Christopher Steele of Orbis Business Intelligence.

If you have found this 'handbook' about why Brexit must be 'Halted Now' useful, do please give it a Tweet or a mention on Facebook – today that is indeed how people come to know that a book they want!

Say not the struggle nought availeth,
The labour and the wounds are vain,
The enemy faints not, nor faileth,
And as things have been they remain.

If hopes were dupes, fears may be liars;
It may be, in yon smoke concealed,
Your comrades chase e'en now the fliers,
And, but for you, possess the field.

Arthur Hugh Clough

Here is that remarkable speech which is so little known but is a 'must read' now that Jeremy Corbyn could become the UK's next Prime Minister.

Jeremy Corbyn Leader of the Labour Party:

Speech to Senate House 14 April 2016

The people of this country face a historic choice on 23rd June whether to remain part of the European Union, or to leave. I welcome the fact that that decision is now in the hands of the British people. Indeed, I voted to support a referendum in the last Parliament.

The move to hold this referendum may have been more about managing divisions in the Conservative party. But it is now a crucial democratic opportunity for people to have their say on our country's future, and the future of our continent as a whole.

The Labour Party is overwhelmingly for staying in because we believe the European Union has brought: investment, jobs and protection for workers, consumers and the environment, and offers the best chance of meeting the challenges we face in the 21st century. Labour is convinced that a vote to remain is in the best interests of the people of this country.

In the coming century, we face huge challenges, as a people, as a continent and as a global community. How to deal with climate change. How to address the overweening power of global corporations and ensure they pay fair taxes. How to tackle cyber-crime and terrorism. How to ensure we trade fairly and protect jobs and pay in an era of globalisation. How to address the causes of the huge refugee movements across the world, and how we adapt to a world where people everywhere move more frequently to live, work and retire.

All these issues are serious and pressing, and self-evidently require international co-operation. Collective international action through the European Union is clearly going to be vital to meeting these challenges. Britain will be stronger if we co-operate with our neighbours in facing them together.

As Portugal's new Socialist Prime Minister, Antonio Costa, has said: 'in the face of all these crises around us. We must not divide Europe – we must strengthen it.'

When the last referendum was held in 1975, Europe was divided by the Cold War, and what later became the EU was a much smaller, purely market-driven arrangement. Over the years I have been critical of many decisions taken by the EU, and I remain critical of its shortcomings; from its lack of democratic accountability to the institutional pressure to deregulate or privatise public services.

So Europe needs to change. But that change can only come from working with our allies in the EU. It's perfectly possible to be critical and still be convinced we need to remain a member.

I've even had a few differences with the direction the Labour Party's taken over the past few years but I have been sure that it was right to stay a member some might say I've even managed to do something about changing that direction.

In contrast to four decades ago, the EU of today brings together most of the countries of Europe and has developed important employment, environmental and consumer protections.

I have listened closely to the views of trade unions, environmental groups, human rights organisations and of course to Labour Party members and supporters, and fellow MPs. They are overwhelmingly convinced that we can best make a positive difference by remaining in Europe.

Britain needs to stay in the EU as the best framework for trade, manufacturing and cooperation in 21st century Europe. Tens of billion pounds-worth of investment and millions of jobs are linked to our relationship with the EU, the biggest market in the world.
EU membership has guaranteed working people vital employment rights, including four weeks' paid holiday, maternity and paternity leave, protections for agency workers and health and safety in the workplace. Being in the EU has raised Britain's environmental standards, from beaches to air quality, and protected consumers from rip-off charges.

But we also need to make the case for reform in Europe – the reform David Cameron's Government has no interest in, but plenty of others across Europe do.

That means democratic reform to make the EU more accountable to its people. Economic reform to end to self-defeating austerity and put jobs and sustainable growth at the centre of European policy, labour market reform to strengthen and extend workers' rights in a real social Europe. And new rights for governments and elected authorities to support public enterprise and halt the pressure to privatise services.

So the case I'm making is for 'Remain - and Reform' in Europe.

Today is the Global Day of Action for Fast Food Rights. In the US workers are demanding $15 an hour, in the UK £10 now. Labour is an internationalist party and socialists have understood from the earliest days of the labour movement that workers need to make common cause across national borders.

Working together in Europe has led to significant gains for workers here in Britain and Labour is determined to deliver further progressive reform in 2020 the democratic Europe of social justice and workers' rights that people throughout our continent want to see.

But real reform will mean making progressive alliances across the EU – something that the Conservatives will never do.

Take the crisis in the steel industry. It's a global problem and a challenge to many European governments. So why is it only the British Government that has failed so comprehensively to act to save steel production at home?

The European Commission proposed new tariffs on Chinese steel, but it was the UK Government that blocked these co-ordinated efforts to stop Chinese steel dumping.

Those proposals are still on the table. So today I ask David Cameron and George Osborne to to start sticking up for British steel and work with our willing European partners to secure its future.

There are certainly problems about EU state aid rules, which need reform. But if as the Leave side argues, it is the EU that is the main problem, how is that Germany, Italy, France and Spain have all done so much better at protecting their steel industries?

It is because those countries have acted within EU state aid rules to support their industries; whether through taking a public stake, investing in research and development, providing loan guarantees or compensating for energy costs.

It is not the EU that is the problem, but a Conservative Government here in Britain that doesn't recognise the strategic importance of steel, for our economy and for the jobs and skills in those communities.

The Conservative Government has blocked action on Chinese steel dumping. It has cut investment in infrastructure that would have created demand for more steel and had no procurement strategy to support British steel.

A Labour government would have worked with our partners across Europe to stand up for steel production in Britain.

The European Union – 28 countries and 520 million people – could have made us stronger, by defending our steel industries together. The actions of the Conservative Government weakened us.

The jobs being created under this Government are too often low skill, low pay and insecure jobs. If we harnessed Europe's potential we could be doing far more to defend high skill jobs in the steel industry.

And that goes for other employers of high skilled staff too – from Airbus to Nissan - they have made it clear that their choice to invest in Britain is strengthened by our membership of the European Union.

Of course the Conservatives are loyally committed to protecting one British industry in Europe - the tax avoidance industry.

The most telling revelation about our Prime Minister has not been about his own tax affair, but that in 2013 he personally intervened with the European Commission President to undermine an EU drive to reveal the beneficiaries of offshore trusts, and even now, in the wake of the Panama Papers, he still won't act.

And on six different occasions since the beginning of last year Conservative MEPs have voted down attempts to take action against tax dodging.

Labour has allies across Europe prepared to take on this global network of the corrupt and we will work with them to clamp down on those determined to suck wealth out of our economies and the pockets of our people.

On Tuesday, the EU announced a step forward on country-by-country reporting. We believe we can go further. But even this modest measure was opposed by Conservative MEPs last December.

Left to themselves, it is clear what the main Vote Leave vision is for Britain to be the safe haven of choice for the ill-gotten gains of every dodgy oligarch, dictator or rogue corporation.

They believe this tiny global elite is what matters, not the rest of us, who they dismiss as "low achievers".

Some argue that we need to leave the EU because the single market's rules are driving deregulation and privatisation. They certainly need reform. But it was not the EU that privatised our railways. It was the Conservative Government of John Major and many of our rail routes are now run by other European nations' publicly owned rail companies. They haven't made the mistake of asset stripping their own countries.

Labour is committed to bringing rail back into public ownership in 2020. And that is why Labour MEPs are opposing any element of the fourth rail package, currently before the European Parliament, that might make that more difficult.

The Transatlantic Trade and Investment Partnership is also a huge cause for concern, but we defeated a similar proposal before in Europe, together when it was called the Multilateral Agreement on Investment, back in 1998.

Labour MEPs are rightly opposing the Investor-State Dispute Mechanism opposing any attempt to enforce privatisation on our public services, to reduce consumer rights, workplace protections or environmental standards.

The free market enthusiasts in the Leave campaign would put all those protections at risk. Labour is building alliances to safeguard them.

We must also put human rights at the centre of our trade agreements, not as an optional add-on. We already have allies across Europe to do that. And the EU is vital for promoting human rights at home. As a result of EU directives and regulations, disabled people are protected from discrimination. Lifts, cars and buses need to be accessible, as does sea and air travel.

And it was the Labour Government that signed the Human Rights Act into UK law that transferred power from government – not to Brussels – but to individual citizens.

Climate change is the greatest threat that humanity faces this century. And Britain cannot tackle it alone. We could have the best policies possible but unless we act together internationally, it is worthless. Labour brought in the Climate Change Act, John Prescott played a key role in getting the Kyoto Protocols agreed. Labour has led the debate within Europe.

But despite David Cameron pledging to lead the greenest Government ever, Britain still lags far behind most of Europe in terms of renewable energy production. We have much to learn from what Germany has done in particular.

The Conservative Government has cut subsidies for solar power while increasing subsidies for diesel. It has cut regulatory burdens on fracking yet increased regulations on onshore wind. They say one thing, but do another.

Again, it has been regulations agreed in Europe that have improved Britain's beaches and waterways and that are forcing us to tackle the scandal of air pollution which will kill 500,000 people in Britain by 2025, unless we act.

Working together in the European Union is vital for tackling climate change and vital in protecting the environment we share.

No doubt debate about EU membership in the next couple of months will focus strongly on jobs and migration. We live in an increasingly globalised world. Many of us will study, work or even retire abroad at some point in our lives.

Free movement has created opportunities for British people. There are nearly three-quarters of a million British people living in Spain and over two million living in the EU as a whole.

Learning abroad and working abroad, increases the opportunities and skills of British people and migration brings benefits as well as challenges at home.

But it's only if there is government action to train enough skilled workers to stop the exploitation of migrant labour to undercut wages and invest in local services and housing in areas of rapid population growth that they will be felt across the country.

And this Government has done nothing of the sort. Instead, its failure to train enough skilled workers means we have become reliant on migration to keep our economy functioning.

This is especially true of our NHS which depends on migrant nurses and doctors to fill vacancies. This Government has failed to invest in training, and its abolition of nurses' bursaries, and its decision to pick a fight with junior doctors is likely to make those shortages worse.

As a former representative of NHS workers, I value our NHS and admire the dedication of all its staff. It is Labour's proudest creation. But right now, it would be in even greater crisis if many on the Leave side had their way. Some of whom have argued against the NHS and free healthcare on demand in principle.

And of course it is EU regulations that that underpin many rights at work, like holiday entitlement, maternity leave, rights to take breaks and limits to how many hours we can work, and that have helped to improve protection for agency workers.

The Tories and UKIP are on record as saying they would like to cut back EU-guaranteed workplace rights if they could.

A Labour government would instead strengthen rights at work making common cause with our allies to raise employment standards throughout Europe, to stop the undercutting of wages and conditions by unscrupulous employers, to strengthen the protection of every worker in Europe.

Just imagine what the Tories would do to workers' rights here in Britain if we voted to leave the EU in June. They'd dump rights on equal pay, working time, annual leave, for agency workers, and on maternity pay as fast as they could get away with it. It would be a bonfire of rights that Labour governments secured within the EU.

Not only that, it wouldn't be a Labour government negotiating a better settlement for working people with the EU. It would be a Tory government, quite possibly led by Boris Johnson and backed by Nigel Farage, that would negotiate the worst of all worlds: a free market free-for-all shorn of rights and protections.

It is sometimes easier to blame the EU, or worse to blame foreigners, than to face up to our own problems. At the head of which right now is a Conservative Government that is failing the people of Britain.

There is nothing remotely patriotic about selling off our country and our national assets to the highest bidder. Or in handing control of our economy to City hedge-funds and tax-dodging corporations based in offshore tax havens.

There is a strong socialist case for staying in the European Union. Just as there is also a powerful socialist case for reform and progressive change in Europe.

That is why we need a Labour government, to stand up – at the European level – for industries and communities in Britain, to back public ownership and public services, to protect and extend workers' rights and to work with our allies to make both Britain and Europe work better for working people.

Many people are still weighing up how they will vote in this referendum. And I appeal to everyone, especially young people – who will live longest with the consequences – to make sure you are registered to vote. And vote to keep Britain in Europe this June. This is about your future.

By working together across our continent, we can develop our economies protect social and human rights, tackle climate change and clamp down on tax dodgers.

You cannot build a better world unless you engage with the world, build allies and deliver change. The EU, warts and all, has proved itself to be a crucial international framework to do that.

That is why I will be am backing Britain to remain in Europe and I hope you will too.

ENDS

The full text of Lord Kerr's lecture of 10 November 2017 is below:

"Article 50 emerged 15 years ago, in a Convention of 200 Parliamentarians from all the countries who then were members of, or were then negotiating to join, the EU. I was their Secretary-General.

"One of their concerns was to demonstrate that the Union was a voluntary partnership of sovereign nation-states, based on treaties between states, not the incipient super-state of Eurosceptic nightmares. Including an Article setting out a procedure for orderly divorce was one of several ways of underlining the voluntary nature of the Union. Though we called our product a Constitutional treaty I can't recall anyone suggesting adding any "We, the People..." claim to a legitimacy going over the heads of elected national governments.

"Nor do I remember any serious opposition to the idea, enshrined in the Lisbon Treaty in what became Article 50, that nation-states were entitled to change their minds, and leave if they so choose. Equally I'm certain no-one dreamed that in 2017 a member state would trigger the procedure, as Mrs. May did on 29 March.

"Now that we're in the procedure, it's important to understand it; and I am concerned that some aspects of the Article seem to me rather inadequately reflected, or indeed misinterpreted, in our current public debate.

"I want to highlight 4 points.

"First, while we're in, we're in. While the divorce talks proceed, the parties are still married. Reconciliation is still possible. The Article requires the parties to negotiate the "arrangements" for our withdrawal; but we are not required to withdraw just because Mrs.

May sent her letter. We can change our minds at any stage during the process.

"Second, however, there is a time-limit. To reassure a member-state wishing to leave that it could not be trapped in endless fruitless negotiation, the Article is clear that after 2 years, one is out. But the time-limit can be extended if all parties consent: this could become important.

"Third, Article 50 is only about divorce. Any Agreement about future relationships, e.g. on trade, between us and the 27 would be negotiated under other Articles, with different voting rules; and could only be concluded after we had left; and, unlike an Art 50 Agreement, would probably require ratification in every member-state, which in some countries would require referendums.

"Fourth, once we're out, we're out. The Article is clear that there can be no keeping a back-door key. If, once we'd left, we were to change our mind, and want to go back in, we would have to go through the full Accession procedure, like any other candidate-country. That would entail paying a price.

"Taking these in turn...

"First, and crucially, as required by the Treaty, Mrs. May's letter was only a notification of the UK's "intention" to withdraw. Intentions can change. We still have all the rights of a member-state, including the right to change our minds and our votes, as member-states frequently do, for example after elections. The Article is about voluntary withdrawal, not about expulsion: we don't have to go if at any stage, within the two years, we decide we don't want to.

"The clause that says that "once we're out, we're out" says just that, and only that. If we had wanted declaring an intention to go to be the Rubicon moment, if we had wanted a notification letter to be irrevocable, we would have drafted the clause to say so. But we didn't, and the clause doesn't. So, the die is not cast irretrievably. The letter can be taken back.

"That has subsequently been confirmed by formidable legal experts. Let me cite just two. Jean-Claude Piris, Legal Counsel to the Council in my Convention days, is clear that "even after triggering Article 50, and notifying the EU of its intention to leave, there is no legal obstacle to the UK changing its mind." Sir David Edward, UK Judge in the ECJ when the Article was drafted, says the same.

"The Government give the impression that the Rubicon has been crossed, but they currently refuse to publish their Law Officers' Opinion: I think we know why. They have been careful not to say that we could not take back Mrs. May's letter. During the Miller case, and at the Despatch Box in both Houses, Government spokesmen have consistently said only that "as a matter of firm policy ", we won't take it back. That formula in itself confirms that we could take it back.

"The fact is that a political decision has been made, in this country, to maintain that there can be no going back. Actually, the country still has a free choice about whether to proceed. As new facts emerge, people are entitled to take a different view. And there's nothing in Article 50 to stop them. I think the British people have the right to know this – they should not be misled.

"Supposing we were to exercise our right to withdraw Mrs. May's letter, how would leaders across the Channel react? We know from what they have said: they would applaud. Let me cite a couple of Presidents...

"If the UK wanted to stay, everybody would be in favour. I would be very happy."

That's Antonio Tajani, President of the European Parliament.

"It is in fact up to London how this will end: with a good deal, no deal, or no Brexit."

That's Donald Tusk, President of the European Council.

"Or take the Taoiseach, Leo Varadkar ... "The door remains open for the UK to stay in the EU." Yes. It does.

And President Macron has said the same.

"Most EU leaders think Brexit would be a disaster, worst for us, but bad for all. Most believe that, in a world of Trump and Putin, of Daesh and Islamic State, of Asian competition, of climate change and migration misery, Europe should stick together and work together. They of course recognise that we have every right to take a different view, but they hope that in the end we won't. They value our contribution to the Union's vitality, remembering with respect how Mrs. Thatcher fought to create the Single Market, and John Major and Tony Blair insisted, when the Wall came down, that we must bring in the new democracies of Central and Eastern Europe.

"They often find us difficult partners, annoyingly pragmatic and practical. But they now find us puzzlingly dogmatic and doctrinaire on Brexit. If we were to change our minds, Putin and Trump would be disappointed, but our near neighbours, and our true friends across the Atlantic and in the Commonwealth, would cheer. I think the country should know that.

"My second concern is less fundamental, but I am uneasy that the country isn't being told much about the possibility of taking more time.

"I don't know why Mrs. May was in such a rush to send her letter in March, before her Cabinet had an agreed plan. It was odd to start the clock and not start negotiating, instead calling an Election. And I don't know why both Government and Opposition now seem to discount the possibility of our seeking an extension. Predicting how the 27 would react to such a request is harder than predicting how they would react to our withdrawing the letter, and if anyone refused there would be no extension. I believe much would depend on our perceived motive. If we were seen as simply wanting to take a deadlocked financial negotiation into Extra Time, I doubt if we could be sure of the necessary unanimous consent.

"But if, for example, we were to need time for Parliament to consider a final deal, an Election, and/or to pass the legislation needed for a referendum giving the people the final say on this process, to check that the country, having seen the facts emerge during the negotiation process, still wanted to Leave, I do not see any of 27 democracies denying us the chance to consult the people. They would think we had every right to check that the country, by then aware of the facts, still wanted to Leave. How the people should be consulted at the end of this negotiation process is an issue for the politicians not me, but the country is entitled to know that different options are open to it.

"My third concern is over confusion about "transitions", "implementation periods", "standstills", and cliff-edges.

"I believe it was unwise of the 27 to insist on "sufficient progress" on money before turning to the future relationship. I think they were wrong to be misled by suggestions here that they could "go whistle", and that we might refuse to honour our commitments: I'm sure we never would. And it would of course be self-defeating: lengthy arbitration or court proceedings about unpaid bills would severely complicate full WTO accession. I believe that there should now be parallel tracks, one looking back, on settling debts, one looking forward, on future partnership plans, everything on the understanding that nothing can be finally agreed on either until all is agreed on both. I hope that will now happen.

"But I am puzzled by UK suggestions that a fully comprehensive agreement about the future can be completed and initialed by this time next year. EU trade agreements with third countries come under Article 218, not Article 50. They take time, and Association agreements take longer. And getting widely-drawn agreements ratified can be tricky: the Canadian negotiations have taken 7 years, and I hope that a UK/EU agreement would go wider, extending beyond Goods into Services. And ratifying widely-drawn agreements can be problematic: the Canadian deal got stuck in the Wallonian parliament.

"But we, the Article 50 drafters, had thought of the timing problem: hence the stipulation in the Article that the divorce settlement must be drawn up "taking account of the framework for the future relationship with the Union." When will we at last put forward a draft framework, a "Heads of Agreement " text, the basis for an agreed outline, or set of principles, which would guide the subsequent detailed sectoral negotiations? And why do we insist that the ball is in the EU court? Having service is usually seen as conferring an advantage. The best time to submit our ideas for the framework might have been before starting the 2-year clock. But better late than never.

"And do we really envisage that by next October we shall have not only initialed a permanent agreement, but will have also, subsequently, reached agreement on a transitional regime to get us from here to there, so avoiding the cliff-edge in 2019? This seems no less puzzling. Since we won't have a clear picture of the detail of future permanent arrangements, I don't see how we could build a bridge to them. Without some framework, we risk having nothing to "transition" to, nothing to "implement".

"In her Florence speech Mrs. May seemed to acknowledge this, and floated instead the idea of a standstill, for some two years, during which we would, after Leaving, continue to apply all EU rules and regulations. The 27 have in fact offered that from the start: their April Guidelines say that " should a time-limited prolongation of Union acquis be considered, this would require all existing Union regulatory, budgetary, supervisory, judiciary, and enforcement instruments and structures to apply." In Florence, it sounded as if Mrs. May might buy all that, for two or three years. But subsequent statements by Mr. Johnson, Dr. Fox and Mr. Gove suggest that they don't.

"But the key point about such a standstill is that it doesn't avoid the cliff-edge; It merely postpones it for a couple of years. That wouldn't provide the certainty business so badly needs. And whether it's called Transition, Implementation or Standstill, it would follow our Leaving. Once we're out, say in March 2019, we're out, with no votes, no judge, no commissioner, no MEPs, and no way back, other than an Accession negotiation, starting from scratch. Again, I think the country needs to know that.

"My last point can be briefly put. I think the country should also be aware of one big difference between, on the one hand, negotiating for accession, and, on the other, drawing back from secession: in the former, there's a price to pay; in the latter, there isn't.

"If we were eventually to apply to re-join the EU, it might be rather difficult to persuade 27, or by then maybe more, member-states, many of them less wealthy, in per capita terms, than us, that we should have a budget rebate. Mrs. Thatcher secured it from inside, after quite a fight, and it isn't universally -popular. To sell the idea again, from outside, would not be possible.

"Conversely, while we're in, we're in; and there would be no price to pay if we were to decide to stay in. The rebate is part of a legal text known as the Own Resources Decision, which can be amended only if all member-states agree. While we remain a member-state, we would not agree to drop the Rebate. and since we are entitled to remain a member-state, we could not be forced to do so.

"My conclusions are simple.

"The national debate about Brexit should take account of the facts that:

i.   our Article 50 letter could be withdrawn without cost or difficulty, legal or political;

ii.   a standstill agreement is no panacea;

iii.   once out, there is no easy way back in, and there would be a price to pay; but

iv.   while still in, the option of stopping the clock, in order to
consult the people again, is available.

"All four facts will still be relevant when Parliament next autumn gets
the chance, as it must, to assess the outcome of the negotiations."-

=================================

Traduction francaise:-

Le texte intégral du discours de Lord Kerr du 10 novembre 2017 est ci-
dessous:

"L'article 50 a vu le jour il y a 15 ans, dans une convention de 200
parlementaires de tous les pays qui étaient alors membres de l'UE, ou
qui étaient en train de négocier. J'étais leur secrétaire général.

"L'une de leurs préoccupations était de démontrer que l'Union était un
partenariat volontaire d'Etats-nations souverains, fondé sur des traités
entre Etats, et non pas sur le super-état naissant des cauchemars
eurosceptiques. L'inclusion d'un article énonçant une procédure de
divorce ordonné est l'un des moyens de souligner le caractère
volontaire de l'Union. Bien que nous ayons qualifié notre produit de
traité constitutionnel, je ne me souviens pas que quiconque ait suggéré
d'ajouter une revendication de «Nous, les peuples ...» à une légitimité
allant au-delà des gouvernements nationaux élus.

"Je ne me souviens pas non plus d'une opposition sérieuse à l'idée,
inscrite dans le traité de Lisbonne dans ce qui est devenu l'article 50,
que les Etats-nations aient le droit de changer d'avis et de partir s'ils le
souhaitent. De même, je suis certain que personne n'a rêvé qu'en 2017
un État membre déclencherait la procédure, comme Mme May l'a fait
le 29 mars.

"Maintenant que nous sommes dans la procédure, il est important de
le comprendre; et je suis préoccupé par le fait que certains aspects de
l'article me semblent plutôt insuffisamment reflétés, ou même mal
interprétés, dans notre débat public actuel.

"Je veux mettre en évidence 4 points.

«D'abord, pendant que nous sommes dans, nous sommes po Pendant que les pourparlers de divorce avancent, les parties sont toujours mariées. La réconciliation est toujours possible. L'article exige des parties qu'elles négocient les «arrangements» pour notre retrait; mais nous ne sommes pas tenus de nous retirer juste parce que Mme May a envoyé sa lettre. Nous pouvons changer d'avis à n'importe quelle étape du processus.

"Deuxièmement, cependant, il y a un délai. Pour rassurer un Etat membre désireux de partir qu'il ne pourrait pas être piégé dans une négociation sans fin sans fin, l'article est clair qu'après 2 ans, on est sorti. Mais le délai peut être prolongé si toutes les parties y consentent: cela pourrait devenir important.

"Troisièmement, l'article 50 concerne uniquement le divorce. Tout accord sur les relations futures, par ex. sur le commerce, entre nous et les 27 seraient négociés en vertu d'autres articles, avec des règles de vote différentes; et ne pouvait être conclu qu'après notre départ; et, contrairement à un accord de l'article 50, nécessiterait probablement la ratification dans chaque État membre, ce qui dans certains pays nécessiterait des référendums.

"Quatrièmement, une fois que nous sommes sortis, nous sommes sortis. L'article est clair qu'il ne peut y avoir de garder une clé de porte arrière. Si, une fois que nous étions partis, nous devions changer d'avis et que nous voulions y retourner, nous devrions suivre la procédure d'adhésion complète, comme n'importe quel autre pays candidat. Cela impliquerait de payer un prix.

"Prendre ces à son tour ...

"Premièrement, et d'une manière primordiale, comme l'exige le Traité, la lettre de Mme May n'était qu'une notification de" l'intention "du Royaume-Uni de se retirer. Les intentions peuvent changer. Nous avons toujours tous les droits d'un État membre, y compris le droit de changer d'avis et de voter, comme le font fréquemment les États membres, par exemple après les élections. L'article parle de retrait volontaire, pas d'expulsion: nous ne sommes pas obligés d'y aller si, à un moment ou à un autre, nous décidons que nous ne le voulons pas.

"La clause qui dit que" une fois que nous sommes sortis, nous sommes sortis "dit juste cela, et seulement cela. Si nous avions voulu déclarer l'intention d'être le moment Rubicon, si nous avions voulu qu'une lettre de notification soit irrévocable, nous aurions rédigé la clause pour le dire. Mais nous ne l'avons pas fait, et la clause ne l'est pas. Donc, le dé n'est pas coulé irrémédiablement. La lettre peut être reprise.

"Cela a été confirmé par des experts juridiques formidables. Permettez-moi de citer seulement deux. Jean-Claude Piris, Conseiller juridique du Conseil à l'époque de la Convention, dit clairement que «même après avoir déclenché l'article 50 et notifié à l'UE son intention de partir, il n'y a pas d'obstacle légal au Royaume-Uni». Edward, Royaume-Uni juge à la CJE lorsque l'article a été rédigé, dit la même chose.

"Le gouvernement donne l'impression que le Rubicon a été franchi, mais ils refusent actuellement de publier l'avis de leurs avocats: Je pense que nous savons pourquoi. Ils ont pris soin de ne pas dire que nous ne pouvions pas reprendre la lettre de Mme May. Dans l'affaire Miller et dans la boîte d'expédition des deux Chambres, les porte-parole du gouvernement ont toujours dit seulement que «dans le cadre d'une politique ferme», nous ne le reprendrons pas. Cette formule confirme en soi que nous pourrions le reprendre.

"Le fait est qu'une décision politique a été prise, dans ce pays, de soutenir qu'il ne peut y avoir de retour en arrière. En fait, le pays a toujours le choix de poursuivre. À mesure que de nouveaux faits apparaissent, les gens ont le droit d'adopter un point de vue différent. Et rien dans l'article 50 ne les arrête. Je pense que les Britanniques ont le droit de savoir cela - ils ne devraient pas être induits en erreur.

"Supposons que nous devions exercer notre droit de retirer

"Premièrement, et d'une manière primordiale, comme l'exige le Traité, la lettre de Mme May n'était qu'une notification de" l'intention "du

Royaume-Uni de se retirer. Les intentions peuvent changer. Nous avons toujours tous les droits d'un État membre, y compris le droit de changer d'avis et de voter, comme le font fréquemment les États membres, par exemple après les élections. L'article parle de retrait volontaire, pas d'expulsion: nous ne sommes pas obligés d'y aller si, à un moment ou à un autre, nous décidons que nous ne le voulons pas.

"La clause qui dit que" une fois que nous sommes sortis, nous sommes sortis "dit juste cela, et seulement cela. Si nous avions voulu déclarer l'intention d'être le moment Rubicon, si nous avions voulu qu'une lettre de notification soit irrévocable, nous aurions rédigé la clause pour le dire. Mais nous ne l'avons pas fait, et la clause ne l'est pas. Donc, le dé n'est pas coulé irrémédiablement. La lettre peut être reprise.

"Cela a été confirmé par des experts juridiques formidables. Permettez-moi de citer seulement deux. Jean-Claude Piris, Conseiller juridique du Conseil à l'époque de la Convention, dit clairement que «même après avoir déclenché l'article 50 et notifié à l'UE son intention de partir, il n'y a pas d'obstacle légal au Royaume-Uni». Edward, Royaume-Uni juge à la CJE lorsque l'article a été rédigé, dit la même chose.

"Le gouvernement donne l'impression que le Rubicon a été franchi, mais ils refusent actuellement de publier l'avis de leurs avocats: Je pense que nous savons pourquoi. Ils ont pris soin de ne pas dire que nous ne pouvions pas reprendre la lettre de Mme May. Dans l'affaire Miller et dans la boîte d'expédition des deux Chambres, les porte-parole du gouvernement ont toujours dit seulement que «dans le cadre d'une politique ferme», nous ne le reprendrons pas. Cette formule confirme en soi que nous pourrions le reprendre.

"Le fait est qu'une décision politique a été prise, dans ce pays, de soutenir qu'il ne peut y avoir de retour en arrière. En fait, le pays a toujours le choix de poursuivre. À mesure que de nouveaux faits apparaissent, les gens ont le droit d'adopter un point de vue différent. Et rien dans l'article 50 ne les arrête. Je pense que les Britanniques ont le droit de savoir cela - ils ne devraient pas être induits en erreur.

"Supposons que nous devions exercer notre droit de retirer la lettre de Mme May, comment réagiraient les dirigeants d'outre-Manche? Nous savons de ce qu'ils ont dit: ils applaudiraient. Permettez-moi de citer quelques présidents ... "Si le Royaume-Uni voulait rester, tout le monde serait en faveur. Je serais très content."

C'est Antonio Tajani, président du Parlement européen. "C'est en fait à Londres comment cela va se terminer: avec une bonne affaire, pas d'accord, ou pas de Brexit." C'est Donald Tusk, président du Conseil européen. "Ou prenez le Taoiseach, Leo Varadkar ..." La porte reste ouverte pour que le Royaume-Uni reste dans l'UE "Oui, c'est vrai. Et le président Macron a dit la même chose. "La plupart des dirigeants européens pensent que le Brexit serait une catastrophe, pire pour nous, mais mauvaise pour tous. La plupart croient que, dans un monde de Trump et Poutine, de Daech et de l'État islamique, de la concurrence asiatique, du changement climatique et de la misère migratoire, l'Europe devrait rester solidaire et travailler ensemble. Bien sûr, ils reconnaissent que nous avons tous le droit d'adopter un point de vue différent, mais ils espèrent qu'en fin de compte nous ne le ferons pas. Ils apprécient notre contribution à la vitalité de l'Union, se rappelant avec respect comment Mme Thatcher s'est battue pour créer le marché unique, et John Major et Tony Blair ont insisté, quand le mur est tombé, sur l'introduction des nouvelles démocraties d'Europe centrale et orientale. . "Ils nous trouvent souvent des partenaires difficiles, agaçants, pragmatiques et pratiques. Mais ils nous trouvent maintenant curieusement dogmatiques et doctrinaires sur le Brexit. Si nous devions changer d'avis, Poutine et Trump seraient déçus, mais nos voisins proches, et nos vrais amis de l'autre côté de l'Atlantique et du Commonwealth, se réjouiraient. Je pense que le pays devrait le savoir.

"Ma deuxième préoccupation est moins fondamentale, mais je suis inquiète que l'on ne parle pas beaucoup au pays de la possibilité de prendre plus de temps. "Je ne sais pas pourquoi Mme May était si pressée d'envoyer sa lettre en mars, avant que son cabinet ait un plan convenu. C'était bizarre de commencer l'horloge et de ne pas commencer à négocier, au lieu d'appeler une élection. Et je ne sais pas pourquoi le gouvernement et l'opposition semblent maintenant ignorer la possibilité de demander une prolongation. Prédire comment les 27 réagiraient à une telle demande est plus difficile que de prédire comment ils réagiraient à notre retrait de la lettre, et si quelqu'un refusait, il n'y aurait pas de prolongation. Je crois que beaucoup dépendrait de notre motif perçu. Si nous étions perçus comme voulant simplement faire passer une négociation financière dans l'impasse dans les prolongations, je doute que nous puissions être sûrs du consentement unanime nécessaire.

Mais si, par exemple, nous avions besoin de temps pour que le Parlement envisage un accord final, une élection, et / ou d'adopter la législation nécessaire pour un référendum donnant aux gens le dernier mot sur ce processus, de vérifier que le pays, vu les faits émergent au cours du processus de négociation, toujours voulu partir, je ne vois aucune des 27 démocraties qui nous refusent la possibilité de consulter les gens. Ils penseraient que nous avions le droit de vérifier que le pays, alors conscient des faits, voulait toujours partir. La façon dont les gens devraient être consultés à la fin de ce processus de négociation est un problème pour les politiciens, pas pour moi, mais le pays a le droit de savoir que différentes options s'offrent à lui. "Ma troisième préoccupation concerne la confusion au sujet des" transitions ", des" périodes de mise en œuvre ", des" arrêts "et des falaises. "Je crois qu'il était imprudent des 27 d'insister sur" des progrès suffisants "sur l'argent avant de se tourner vers la relation future. Je pense qu'ils ont eu tort d'être induits en erreur par des suggestions ici qu'ils pourraient «siffler», et que nous pourrions refuser d'honorer nos engagements: je suis sûr que nous ne le ferions jamais. Et cela irait bien sûr à l'encontre du but recherché: un long arbitrage ou une procédure judiciaire concernant des factures impayées compliquerait gravement l'adhésion à l'OMC. Je crois qu'il devrait maintenant y avoir des pistes parallèles, une rétrospective, sur le règlement des dettes, une perspective d'avenir, de futurs projets de partenariat, tout étant entendu que rien ne pourra être finalement convenu tant que tout n'aura pas été convenu. J'espère que cela arrivera maintenant

Mais je suis intrigué par les suggestions du Royaume-Uni selon lesquelles un accord complet sur l'avenir peut être complété et paraphé d'ici la fin de l'année prochaine. Les accords commerciaux de l'UE avec des pays tiers relèvent de l'article 218, et non de l'article 50. Ils prennent du temps et les accords d'association prennent plus de temps. Et obtenir des accords largement ratifiés peut être difficile: les négociations canadiennes ont duré sept ans, et j'espère qu'un accord entre le Royaume-Uni et l'UE ira plus loin, allant au-delà des biens et des services. Et entériner des accords très répandus peut être problématique: l'accord canadien s'est retrouvé coincé dans le parlement wallon.

"Mais nous, les rédacteurs de l'article 50, avions pensé au problème du timing: d'où la stipulation dans l'article que le règlement du divorce doit être établi" en tenant compte du cadre de la future relation avec l'Union ". Quand présenterons-nous enfin un projet de cadre, un texte sur les «Chefs d'accord», sur lequel reposera un schéma ou un ensemble de principes convenus, qui guideront les négociations sectorielles détaillées qui suivront? Et pourquoi insistons-nous pour que la balle soit dans le camp de l'UE? Avoir du service est généralement considéré comme conférant un avantage. Le meilleur moment pour soumettre nos idées pour le cadre pourrait avoir été avant de commencer l'horloge de 2 ans. Mais, mieux vaut tard que jamais. "Et envisageons-nous réellement qu'en octobre prochain nous aurons non seulement paraphé un accord permanent, mais que nous aurons aussi, p   ar la suite, trouvé un accord sur un régime transitoire pour nous mener d'ici là, évitant ainsi la falaise en 2019? Cela ne semble pas moins déroutant. Comme nous n'aurons pas une idée précise des détails des futurs arrangements permanents, je ne vois pas comment nous pourrions leur construire un pont. Sans cadre, nous risquons de n'avoir rien à «transiter», rien à «mettre en œuvre».

"Dans son discours à Florence, Mme May a semblé le reconnaître, et a laissé flotter l'idée d'un arrêt, pendant deux ans, au cours duquel, après Leaving, nous continuerions à appliquer toutes les règles et tous les règlements de l'UE. Les 27 ont d'emblée proposé cela: leurs lignes directrices d'avril stipulent que «si une prolongation limitée de l'acquis de l'Union était envisagée, tous les instruments et structures réglementaires, budgétaires, de surveillance, judiciaires et d'application de la " A Florence, on aurait dit que Mme May pouvait acheter tout ça pendant deux ou trois ans. Mais les déclarations subséquentes de M. Johnson, du Dr Fox et de M. Gove suggèrent que ce n'est pas le cas. "Mais le point clé à propos d'un tel arrêt est qu'il n'évite pas le bord de la falaise; Il ne fait que le reporter pour quelques années. Cela ne fournirait pas la certitude dont les entreprises ont tant besoin. Et que ce soit appelé Transition, Implémentation ou Arrêt, cela suivrait notre départ. Une fois que nous sommes sortis, disons en mars 2019, nous sommes sortis, sans aucun vote, aucun juge, aucun commissaire, aucun député européen et aucun retour en arrière, autre qu'une négociation d'adhésion, à partir de zéro. Encore une fois, je pense que le pays doit le savoir.

Mon dernier point peut être brièvement mis. Je pense que le pays devrait aussi être conscient d'une grande différence entre, d'une part, la négociation pour l'adhésion et, d'autre part, le retrait de la sécession: dans le premier, il y a un prix à payer; dans le dernier, il n'y a pas. "Si nous devions finalement demander à rejoindre l'UE, il pourrait être assez difficile de convaincre 27, ou peut-être plus, Etats membres, beaucoup moins riches, par habitant, que nous, que nous devrions avoir un rabais budgétaire. Mme Thatcher l'a obtenu de l'intérieur, après tout un combat, et il n'est pas universellement populaire. Vendre l'idée de nouveau, de l'extérieur, ne serait pas possible. "Inversement, pendant que nous sommes dedans, nous sommes dedans; Le remboursement fait partie d'un texte juridique connu sous le nom de décision sur les ressources propres, qui ne peut être modifié que si tous les États membres sont d'accord. Alors que nous restons membre, nous ne serions pas d'accord pour abandonner le remboursement. et puisque nous avons le droit de rester membre, nous ne pourrions pas être obligés de le faire. "Mes conclusions sont simples. "Le débat national sur le Brexit devrait tenir compte des faits suivants: je. notre lettre de l'article 50 pourrait être retirée sans coût ni difficulté, juridique ou politique; ii. un accord de statu quo n'est pas une panacée; iii. une fois sorti, il n'y a pas de retour facile, et il y aurait un prix à payer; mais iv. tout en continuant, l'option d'arrêter l'horloge, afin de consulter à nouveau les gens, est disponible. "Les quatre faits seront toujours pertinents lorsque le Parlement l'automne prochain aura la chance, comme il se doit, d'évaluer le résultat des négociations".

======================= ================= ===========

German Translation:-

Rede von Lord Kerr vom 10. November 2017

Artikel 50 entstand vor 15 Jahren in einem Konvent von 200 Parlamentariern aus allen Ländern, die damals Mitglieder der EU waren oder damals verhandelten. Ich war ihr Generalsekretär.

Eines ihrer Anliegen war es zu zeigen, dass die Union eine freiwillige Partnerschaft souveräner Nationalstaaten ist, die sich auf Verträgen zwischen Staaten basiert, und nicht auf dem beginnenden Superstaat der euroskeptischen Albträume. Die Aufnahme eines Artikels, der ein Verfahren für eine ordnungsgemäße Scheidung vorsieht, war eine von mehreren Möglichkeiten, die Freiwilligkeit der Union zu unterstreichen. Obwohl wir unser Produkt als Verfassungsvertrag bezeichneten, kann ich mich an niemanden erinnern, der vorschlägt, „Wir, die Menschen..." würden eine Legitimität über die Köpfe der gewählten nationalen Regierungen hinzufügen.

Ich erinnere mich auch nicht an eine ernsthafte Opposition gegen die Idee, die im Vertrag von Lissabon in Artikel 50 verankert wurde, dass die Nationalstaaten berechtigt waren, ihre Meinung zu ändern und zu gehen, wenn sie das wollten. Ebenso bin ich mir sicher, dass niemand geträumt hat, dass 2017 ein Mitgliedstaat das Verfahren auslösen würde, wie es Frau May am 29. März getan hat.

Jetzt, wo wir im Verfahren sind, ist es wichtig, es zu verstehen; und ich bin besorgt, dass einige Aspekte des Artikels in unserer gegenwärtigen öffentlichen Debatte eher unzureichend reflektiert oder falsch interpretiert werden.

Ich möchte 4 Punkte hervorheben.

Zuerst, solange wir drinnen sind, sind wir dabei. Während die Scheidungsgespräche weitergehen, sind die Parteien immer noch verheiratet. Versöhnung ist noch möglich. Der Artikel verpflichtet die Parteien, die „Vereinbarungen" für unseren Rückzug auszuhandeln; aber wir müssen nicht zurücktreten, nur weil Frau May ihren Brief geschickt hat. Wir können unsere Meinung in jedem Zeitpunkt des Prozesses ändern.

Zweitens gibt es jedoch ein Zeitlimit. Um einen Mitgliedsstaat, der gehen möchte, zu beruhigen, dass er nicht in endlosen fruchtlosen Verhandlungen gefangen sein könnte, ist der Artikel klar, dass man nach 2 Jahren draußen ist. Die Frist kann jedoch verlängert werden, wenn alle Parteien zustimmen: Dies könnte wichtig werden.

Drittens geht es in Artikel 50 nur um die Scheidung. Irgendeine Vereinbarung über zukünftige Beziehungen, z.B. über den Handel würden zwischen uns und den 27 Mitgliedstaaten im Rahmen anderer Artikel mit unterschiedlichen Abstimmungsregeln verhandelt werden; und konnte nur geschlossen werden, nach unser abgereise; Im Gegensatz zu einem Art-50-Abkommen würde in jedem Mitgliedstaat wahrscheinlich eine Ratifizierung erforderlich sein, was in einigen Ländern ein Referendum erfordern würde.

Viertens, wenn wir draußen sind, sind wir draußen. Der Artikel ist klar, dass es keinen Hintertürschlüssel geben kann. Wenn wir nach unserer Abreise unsere Meinung ändern und wieder hineingehen wollen, müssen wir wie alle anderen Bewerberländer das gesamte Beitrittsverfahren durchlaufen. Das würde bedeuten, einen Preis zu zahlen.

Nehmen Sie diese Punkte in der Reihe nach...

Vor allem und im Einklang mit dem Vertrag war das Schreiben von Frau May lediglich eine Mitteilung über die „Absicht" des Vereinigten Königreichs, sich zurückzuziehen. Absichten können sich ändern. Wir haben immer noch alle Rechte eines Mitgliedsstaates, einschließlich des Rechts, unsere Meinung und unsere Stimmen zu ändern, wie es die Mitgliedstaaten häufig tun, zum Beispiel nach Wahlen. Der Artikel handelt von freiwilligem Rückzug, nicht von Ausweisung: Wir müssen nicht gehen, wenn wir irgendwann innerhalb der zwei Jahre entscheiden, dass wir nicht wollen.

Die Klausel, die besagt, dass „wenn wir draußen sind, sind wir draußen", sagt genau das, und nur das. Wenn wir die Absicht haben wollten, zum Rubikon-Moment zu werden, wenn wir gewollt hätten, dass ein Benachrichtigungsschreiben unwiderruflich wäre, hätten wir die Klausel in diesem Sinne entworfen. Aber wir haben es nicht getan, und die Klausel wurde nicht als solch verfasst. Der Würfel wird also nicht unwiederbringlich geworfen. Der Brief kann zurückgenommen werden.

Das wurde später von hervorragenden Rechtsexperten bestätigt. Lassen Sie mich nur zwei nennen. Jean-Claude Piris, Rechtsberater des Rates in meinen Tagen der Konvents, es ist klar, dass „selbst nach der Auslösung von Artikel 50 und der Mitteilung der EU an seine Absicht, sie zu verlassen, es gibt kein Rechtshindernis für das Vereinigte Königreich um seine Meinung zu ändern". Sir David Edward, britischer Richter im EuGH, als der Artikel entworfen wurde, sagt dasselbe.

Die Regierung gibt den Eindruck, dass der Rubikon überschritten wurde, aber sie weigern sich derzeit, die Stellungnahme ihrer Anwälte zu veröffentlichen: Ich denke, wir wissen warum. Sie haben darauf geachtet, nicht zu sagen, dass wir Frau Mays Brief nicht zurücknehmen könnten. Während des Miller-Falles und der Versandbox in beiden Häusern haben die Sprecher der Regierung immer nur gesagt, dass wir „als eine feste Politik" es nicht zurücknehmen werden. Diese Formel bestätigt, dass wir sie zurücknehmen könnten.

Tatsache ist, dass in diesem Land eine politische Entscheidung getroffen wurde, und behaupten dass es kein Zurück mehr gibt. Eigentlich hat das Land noch freie Wahl, ob es weitergehen soll oder nicht. Wenn neue Fakten auftauchen, haben die Menschen ein Recht auf eine andere Sichtweise. Und es gibt nichts in Artikel 50, um sie zu stoppen. Ich denke, dass die Briten das Recht haben, dies zu wissen - sie sollten nicht getäuscht werden.

Angenommen, wir würden von unserem Recht Gebrauch machen, Frau Mays Brief zurückzuziehen, wie würden die Staats- und Regierungschefs jenseits des Kanal reagieren? Wir wissen aus dem, was sie gesagt haben: Sie würden applaudieren. Lassen Sie mich ein paar Präsidenten zitieren...

„Wenn Großbritannien bleiben wollte, wäre jeder dafür. Ich wäre sehr glücklich".
Das ist Antonio Tajani, Präsident des Europäischen Parlaments.

„Es ist in der Tat in London, wie das enden wird: mit einem guten Deal, ohne Deal oder ohne Brexit".
Das ist Donald Tusk, Präsident des Europäischen Rates.

Oder nehmen Sie den Taoiseach (Irischer Premierminister), Leo Varadkar ... „Die Tür bleibt offen, damit das Vereinigte Königreich in der EU bleiben kann. Ja. Das stimmt".
Und Präsident Macron hat dasselbe gesagt.

Die meisten EU-Politiker sind der Ansicht, dass der Brexit eine Katastrophe wäre, am schlimmsten für uns, aber schlecht für alle. Die meisten glauben, dass Europa in einer Welt von Trump und Putin, von Daesh und Islamischem Staat, von asiatischer Konkurrenz, von Klimawandel und Migrationselend, zusammen bleiben und zusammenarbeiten sollte. Sie erkennen natürlich, dass wir jedes Recht haben, eine andere Meinung zu vertreten, aber sie hoffen, dass wir es am Ende nicht tun werden. Sie schätzen unseren Beitrag zur Vitalität der Union und erinnern mit Respekt daran, wie Frau Thatcher für die gründung des Binnenmarktes gekämpft hat, und John Major und Tony Blair bestanden darauf, dass wir nach dem Fall der Mauer die neuen Demokratien in Mittel- und Osteuropa einbringen müssen.

Sie finden uns oft schwierige Partner, ärgerlich pragmatisch und praktisch. Aber sie finden uns jetzt rätselhaft dogmatisch und doktrinär über Brexit. Wenn wir unsere Meinung ändern würden, wären Putin und Trump enttäuscht, aber unsere nahen Nachbarn und unsere wahren Freunde über den Atlantik und im Commonwealth würden uns bejubeln. Ich denke, das Land sollte das wissen.

Meine zweite Sorge ist weniger fundamental, aber ich bin beunruhigt, dass dem Land nicht viel über die Möglichkeit erzählt wird, sich mehr Zeit zu nehmen.

Ich weiß nicht, warum Frau May es eilig hatte, ihren Brief im März zu schicken, bevor ihr Kabinett einen vereinbarten Plan hatte. Es war seltsam, die Uhr zu starten und nicht zu verhandeln, sondern eine Wahl zu rufen. Und ich weiß nicht, warum sowohl die Regierung als auch die Opposition jetzt die Möglichkeit unseres Wunsches nach Verlängerung ausschließen. Die Vorhersage, wie die 27 auf eine solche Anfrage reagieren würde, ist schwieriger als die Vorhersage, wie sie auf unseren Rückzug reagieren würden. Wenn jemand dies verweigern würde, würde es keine Verlängerung geben. Ich glaube viel würde von unserem wahrgenommenen Motiv abhängen. Wenn wir nur eine festgefahrene finanzielle Verhandlung in die Verlängerung aufnehmen wollten, bezweifle ich, ob wir uns der notwendigen einstimmigen Zustimmung sicher sein können.

Aber wenn wir zum Beispiel Zeit brauchen würden, damit das Parlament ein endgültiges Abkommen, eine Wahl und/oder die für ein Referendum notwendigen Gesetze verabschiedet, die den Menschen das letzte Wort über diesen Prozess geben, um zu überprüfen, dass das Land, nach Kenntnisnahme der Faktenlage die während des Verhandlungsprozesses auftauchen, wollten wir immer noch gehen, sehe ich keine der 27 Demokratien, die uns die Möglichkeit verweigern, die Menschen zu befragen. Sie würden denken, wir hätten jedes Recht zu überprüfen, dass das Land, das bis dahin die Fakten kannte, immer noch gehen wollte. Wie die Menschen am Ende dieses Verhandlungsprozesses konsultiert werden sollten, ist ein Problem für die Politiker, nicht für mich, aber das Land hat das Recht zu wissen, dass ihm verschiedene Optionen offen stehen.

Meine dritte Sorge betrifft die Verwirrung über „Übergänge", „Implementierungsperioden", „Stillstände" und „Cliff-Edge"(ohne Vereinbarung verlassen).

Ich glaube, es war unklug von den 27, auf „ausreichendem Fortschritt" beim Geld zu bestehen, bevor sie sich der zukünftigen Beziehung zuwandten. Ich glaube, sie irrten sich unwissentlich durch Vorschläge, dass sie „pfeifen" könnten und dass wir uns weigern würden, unsere Verpflichtungen zu erfüllen: Ich bin mir sicher, dass wir das nie tun würden. Und es würde uns nur selbst schaden: Lange Arbitration oder Gerichtsverfahren über unbezahlte Rechnungen würden den vollen WTO-

218

Beitritt erheblich erschweren. Ich glaube, dass es jetzt parallele Wege geben sollte, von denen man zurückblickt, auf die Begleichung von Schulden, auf zukünftige Partnerschaftspläne, alles in dem Wissen, dass letztlich auch nichts mehr zu vereinbaren ist, bis alles auf beide abgestimmt ist. Ich hoffe, das wird jetzt passieren.

Ich bin jedoch erstaunt über die Vorschläge des Vereinigten Königreichs, dass bis zu diesem Zeitpunkt im nächsten Jahr eine umfassende Vereinbarung über die Zukunft abgeschlossen und paraphiert werden kann. EU-Handelsabkommen mit Drittländern fallen unter Artikel 218, nicht Artikel 50. Sie brauchen Zeit, und Assoziierungsabkommen dauern länger. Und es kann knifflig sein, weit gefasste Abkommen ratifizieren zu lassen: Die Verhandlungen in Kanada haben sieben Jahre gedauert, und ich hoffe, dass ein Abkommen zwischen Großbritannien und der EU weiter hinaus gehen wird als nur Waren und Dienstleistungen. Und die Ratifizierung weit gefasster Vereinbarungen kann problematisch sein: Der kanadische Deal blieb im wallonischen Parlament stecken.

Aber wir, die Verfasser von Artikel 50, hatten an das Timing-Problem gedacht: Daher muss in dem Artikel festgelegt werden, dass die Scheidungsvereinbarung unter „Berücksichtigung des Rahmens für die künftigen Beziehungen zur Union erstellt werden muss". Wann werden wir endlich einen Entwurf für einen Rahmen, einen Text des „Heads of Agreement", die Grundlage für einen vereinbarten Entwurf oder eine Reihe von Grundsätzen, die die nachfolgenden detaillierten sektoralen Verhandlungen leiten würden? Und warum bestehen wir darauf, dass der Ball im EU-Gericht ist? Aufschlag zu haben wird normalerweise als Vorteil angesehen. Die beste Zeit, um unsere Ideen für den Rahmen einzureichen, war möglicherweise vor Beginn der 2-Jahres-Uhr. Aber besser spät als nie.

Und stellen wir uns wirklich vor, dass wir bis zum nächsten Oktober nicht nur ein dauerhaftes Abkommen paraphieren, sondern uns in der Folge auch auf ein Übergangsregime geeinigt haben, um uns von hier nach dort zu bringen und 2019 die „Cliff-Edge" zu umgehen? Dies scheint nicht weniger rätselhaft. Da wir kein klares Bild von den Einzelheiten der zukünftigen dauerhaften Vereinbarungen haben werden, sehe ich nicht, wie wir ihnen eine Brücke bauen könnten. Ohne einen gewissen Rahmen riskieren wir, nichts zu „überführen", nichts zu „implementieren".

In ihrer Rede in Florenz schien Frau May dies anzuerkennen und schwebte stattdessen für zwei Jahre die Idee eines Stillstands vor, während der wir nach dem Austritt weiterhin alle EU-Vorschriften und -Verordnungen anwenden würden. Die 27 haben dies von Anfang an angeboten: In ihren April-Leitlinien heißt es: „Sollte eine zeitlich befristete Verlängerung des Besitzstands der Union in Betracht gezogen werden, müssten alle bestehenden Regulierungs-, Haushalts-, Aufsichts-, Justiz- und Durchsetzungsinstrumente und -strukturen der Union Anwendung finden". In Florenz klang es so, als würde Frau May das alles für zwei oder drei Jahre kaufen. Aber nachfolgende Aussagen von Herr Johnson, Arzt. Fox und Herr Gove deuten darauf hin, dass dies nicht der Fall ist.

Aber der entscheidende Punkt bei einem solchen Stillstand ist, dass er die „Cliff-Edge" nicht meidet; es verschiebt es lediglich um ein paar Jahre. Das würde nicht die so dringende benötigen Rechtssicherheit bringen. Und ob es Übergang, Implementierung oder Stillstand heißt, es würde unserem Weggehen folgen. Wenn wir im März 2019 draußen sind, sind wir draußen, ohne Stimmen, keinen Richter, keinen Kommissar, keine Abgeordneten und keinen Weg zurück, außer einer Beitrittsverhandlung, die von Null beginnt. Ich denke, das Land muss das wissen.

Mein letzter Punkt kann kurz gesagt werden. Ich denke, das Land sollte sich auch eines großen Unterschieds bewusst sein, einerseits zwischen den Beitrittsverhandlungen und andererseits dem Rückzug aus der Sezession: in der einen gibt es einen Preis zu zahlen; in letzterem gibt es nicht.

Wenn wir uns schließlich bewerben würden, um der EU wieder beizutreten, könnte es ziemlich schwierig sein, 27, oder vielleicht sogar mehr, Mitgliedstaaten, von denen viele weniger wohlhabend sind, pro Kopf zu überreden, dass wir es tun sollten einen Budget-Rabatt haben. Frau Thatcher hat es nach einem heftigen Kampf von innen gesichert, und es ist nicht allgemein beliebt. Die Idee von außen wieder zu verkaufen, wäre nicht möglich.

Umgekehrt, während wir drin sind, sind wir drin; und es gäbe keinen Preis zu zahlen, wenn wir uns entscheiden würden, zu bleiben. Der Rabatt ist Teil eines Rechtstextes, der so genannte Eigenmittelbeschluss, der nur geändert werden kann, wenn alle Mitgliedstaaten zustimmen. Während wir ein Mitgliedstaat bleiben, würden wir nicht zustimmen, den Rabatt fallen zu lassen. Und da wir berechtigt sind, ein Mitgliedstaat zu bleiben, könnten wir nicht dazu gezwungen werden.

Meine Schlussfolgerungen sind einfach.
Die nationale Debatte über den Brexit sollte die volgende Fakten berücksichtigen,

i.   unser Schreiben nach Artikel 50 könnte ohne rechtliche oder politische Kosten oder Schwierigkeiten zurückgezogen werden;

ii.   ein Stillstandsabkommen ist kein Allheilmittel;

iii.   Einmal gibt es keinen einfachen Weg zurück, und es würde einen Preis zu zahlen geben; aber

iv.   währenddessen ist die Option verfügbar, die Uhr anzuhalten, um die Leute erneut zu befragen.

„Alle vier Fakten werden immer noch relevant sein, wenn das Parlament im nächsten Herbst die Chance erhält, das Ergebnis der Verhandlungen zu bewerten".

Narcissistic personality disorder (NPD)

- Symptoms & causes
- Diagnosis & treatment

Overview

Narcissistic personality disorder — one of several types of personality disorders — is a mental condition in which people have an inflated sense of their own importance, a deep need for excessive attention and admiration, troubled relationships, and a lack of empathy for others. But behind this mask of extreme confidence lies a fragile self-esteem that's vulnerable to the slightest criticism.

A narcissistic personality disorder causes problems in many areas of life, such as relationships, work, school or financial affairs. People with narcissistic personality disorder may be generally unhappy and disappointed when they're not given the special favors or admiration they believe they deserve. They may find their relationships unfulfilling, and others may not enjoy being around them.

Treatment for narcissistic personality disorder centers around talk therapy (psychotherapy).

Symptoms

Signs and symptoms of narcissistic personality disorder and the severity of symptoms vary. People with the disorder can:

- Have an exaggerated sense of self-importance

- Have a sense of entitlement and require constant, excessive admiration

- Expect to be recognized as superior even without achievements that warrant it

- Exaggerate achievements and talents

- Be preoccupied with fantasies about success, power, brilliance, beauty or the perfect mate

- Believe they are superior and can only associate with equally special people

- Monopolize conversations and belittle or look down on people they perceive as inferior

- Expect special favors and unquestioning compliance with their expectations

- Take advantage of others to get what they want

- Have an inability or unwillingness to recognize the needs and feelings of others

- Be envious of others and believe others envy them

- Behave in an arrogant or haughty manner, coming across as conceited, boastful and pretentious

- Insist on having the best of everything — for instance, the best car or office

At the same time, people with narcissistic personality disorder have trouble handling anything they perceive as criticism, and they can:

- Become impatient or angry when they don't receive special treatment

- Have significant interpersonal problems and easily feel slighted

- React with rage or contempt and try to belittle the other person to make themselves appear superior

- Have difficulty regulating emotions and behavior

- Experience major problems dealing with stress and adapting to change

- Feel depressed and moody because they fall short of perfection

- Have secret feelings of insecurity, shame, vulnerability and humiliation

When to see a doctor

People with narcissistic personality disorder may not want to think that anything could be wrong, so they may be unlikely to seek treatment. If they do seek treatment, it's more likely to be for symptoms of depression, drug or alcohol use, or another mental health problem. But perceived insults to self-esteem may make it difficult to accept and follow through with treatment.

If you recognize aspects of your personality that are common to narcissistic personality disorder or you're feeling overwhelmed by sadness, consider reaching out to a trusted doctor or mental health provider. Getting the right treatment can help make your life more rewarding and enjoyable.

Request an Appointment at Mayo Clinic
Causes

It's not known what causes narcissistic personality disorder. As with personality development and with other mental health disorders, the cause of narcissistic personality disorder is likely complex. Narcissistic personality disorder may be linked to:

- **Environment** — mismatches in parent-child relationships with either excessive adoration or excessive criticism that is poorly attuned to the child's experience

- **Genetics** — inherited characteristics

- **Neurobiology** — the connection between the brain and behavior and thinking

Risk factors

Narcissistic personality disorder affects more males than females, and it often begins in the teens or early adulthood. Keep in mind that, although some children may show traits of narcissism, this may simply be typical of their age and doesn't mean they'll go on to develop narcissistic personality disorder.

Although the cause of narcissistic personality disorder isn't known, some researchers think that in biologically vulnerable children, parenting styles that are overprotective or neglectful may have an impact. Genetics and neurobiology also may play a role in development of narcissistic personality disorder.

Complications

Complications of narcissistic personality disorder, and other conditions that can occur along with it, can include:

- Relationship difficulties

- Problems at work or school

- Depression and anxiety

- Physical health problems

- Drug or alcohol misuse

- Suicidal thoughts or behavior

Prevention

Because the cause of narcissistic personality disorder is unknown, there's no known way to prevent the condition.

==

About the author

John Pedler joined the British Foreign Service – now the Diplomatic
Service - in 1951 when Clement Attlee was to be succeeded by
Winston Churchill (his second Administration). In Europe he served in
Vienna and in Paris where he worked to the Minister of State Edward
Heath when Heath was seeking the UK's membership of the European
Economic Community, now the European Union.

On a year's leave of absence he was war correspondent in Vietnam for
the Sunday Telegraph in 1968, the year of the Têt offensive. On leaving
the Service to become a diplomatic consultant he worked in Germany
on the East West division of the country; was involved with the
Chinese economy paying frequent visits to Mao's China; visited Fidel
Castro's Cuba for discussions with the government; was invited to
Cambodia after the Khmer Rouge genocide by Prime Minister Hun Sen
and became co-founder of the Cambodia Trust; during the siege of
Sarajevo he worked for the Bosnian Government.

Since November 2015 he has worked full time to assist the 'Remain'
organisations, and after the June 30 referendum 2016 he has worked
to support those attempting to prevent Prime Minister Theresa May
from invoking Article 50 of the Lisbon Treaty.

He is the author of 'Our Broken World' and four spy stories. He lives
with his wife in South West France enjoying swimming and
international poetry.

www.ingramcontent.com/pod-product-compliance
Lightning Source LLC
Chambersburg PA
CBHW062140280526
45788CB00001B/246